BLACK SEA

CASPIAN SEA

NOR

Site of Nineveh

SYRIA

R. Tigris

R. Euphrates

Jerusalem

MESOPOTAMIA

P E R S I A

Babylon

• Persepolis

EA

PERSIAN GULF

# The Greeks

# The Greeks

## Kenneth Dover

from the BBC television series by
Christopher Burstall and Kenneth Dover

*British Broadcasting Corporation*

Published by the
British Broadcasting Corporation
35 Marylebone High Street
London W1M 4AA

ISBN 0 563 17805 1

First published 1980
©Sir Kenneth Dover 1980
©Introduction Christopher Burstall 1980

Printed in England by
Butler & Tanner Ltd, Frome and London

# Contents

CONTENTS

# Introduction

## How The Greeks began

The first film in the four-part BBC1 series, *The Greeks*, is called 'The Greek Beginning', and one of the great joys of making television documentaries is that each film is a fresh start and each, even when it is finished, remains a *beginning*. Now the series is made I hope that it, like Kenneth Dover's book, will be a beginning for other people too.

'Oh, it's ancient history,' some will say, 'dead and gone.' But the very word *history* is Greek: it means *enquiry*. *The Greeks* itself was an enquiry, and I worked on the film series for nearly two years, trying to find out how our culture, the kind of people we are and the way we live, are determined by ancient Greek culture, the thought, feelings and deeds of Mediterranean people living nearly two and a half thousand years ago.

I visited many leading Greek scholars, including Geoffrey Lloyd, whom I knew from student days and who is now Reader in Ancient Philosophy and Science at Cambridge, and the late Professor E. R. Dodds, who had been Regius Professor of Greek at Oxford and whose book *The Greeks and the Irrational* opened my eyes to crucial aspects of Greek culture and our own. They and their colleagues all welcomed the idea of a television series, and gradually a feasible and worthwhile television project began to take shape.

Kenneth Dover was among the scholars I went to see. We talked at length. He is one of a distinguished handful of people, highly regarded by leaders in the whole field of Greek studies, linguistics, literature, art and philosophy. What impressed me most at our first meeting was his fair-mindedness.

A sense of fairness is something that most of us have, though whether or not we manage to live by its is another matter. Most of us certainly do not have minds as clear and penetrating as Kenneth Dover's. His sense of fairness was apparent in everything he said and in his whole manner. It seemed to be both part of his mind and his sensibility. This is not to say that he does not have hobby-horses, like everybody else,

vii

or that he is cold and distant. Those who saw him in the four films will have recognised a man of concern as well as curiosity and conviction. He does not wear his heart on his sleeve but I am glad to count him as a warm and sympathetic friend.

I very much wanted *The Greeks* to be fair, for so much that is vague and high-flown has been said and written about ancient Greek achievements. Some weeks after our first exploratory talk we met again. Over several long working sessions we pooled our ideas and established our sticking points. Documentary film-making is a lengthy, organic and complicated process. Once we were properly under way I should be working full-time on the films, but our collaboration could not be full-time: he had his academic life to lead and would neither be available, nor needed, during the months of editing when I should each day be taking decisions about the basic structure of the four films, as well as detailed cutting points. *The Greeks* from the outset seemed to me like a journey of exploration—it finally bore the sub-title, 'A Journey in Space and Time'—and it was necessary to find an approach that we both liked, that would leave each of us free to put our best foot forward. It would be no good at all if collaboration led to constraint, if the whole operation turned into a halt, three-legged race.

We agreed that the series should be thematic, and that Kenneth Dover should write a framework for it. We continued to exchange ideas, and his framework duly arrived. It was short, spare like an antler. We talked for two days into the small hours, cleared the ground, and began.

For nearly a month we worked together, and I wrote words which pointed to what we both wanted to achieve. There were plenty of misunderstandings, plenty of long arguments and more than a dash of disagreement, for we were approaching the subject and the realisation of four films from very different standpoints. He is first and foremost a scholar, concerned above all with the substance and interpretation of ancient Greek texts. I am a late-comer to the field and wanted to show that what ancient Greeks wrote and made and did matters to all of us.

Much later, he said that with the framework he had been barking up the wrong tree. I think he is wrong about that. We departed from its structure radically but it was an invaluable document. I have it beside me now, an old friend.

Slowly, page by page, the four first working scripts took shape. The framework included extracts from several playwrights. Some corresponded with scenes I had been drawn to, others I read with new pleasure. His selection narrowed our choice, and so did the ideas which had led him to pick one passage rather than another. This setting of limits was essential when we were trying to show in about four hours of television some of the main achievements of Greeks in the Classical Age (the period from 500 BC, roughly, to the death of Alexander the Great in

323 BC) and some of the ways in which we are influenced by what men accomplished in that distant span of time.

It seemed to me that we should reduce our number of authors still further, cut out two tragic playwrights altogether, and concentrate on either Aeschylus or Sophocles. We settled for Aeschylus. Pindar and Theocritus had to go. Aristotle kept his place for a long time, but then we crossed out the *Nicomachaean Ethics*. I wanted much more from Thucydides; we agreed on that, and so it went on, line by line, page by page, day by day. We looked at Greek sculpture and vases together, at Assyrian reliefs and Egyptian paintings and I was constantly delighted by the breadth and precision of Kenneth Dover's learning. He has read everything that the ancient Greeks wrote which survives to the present.

One of our jobs, while writing the first scripts, was to plot out scenes where we would be talking together on location. We needed to keep these dialogue scenes open until the actual moment of filming because there would be many more months of work before that time arrived, some of it done jointly during our preliminary travels in Greece, and much of it done separately as the project continued to change and grow in our minds. We agreed that we would each be separately responsible for what we said in the films, and that I should write the film commentary and narrative for the series.

When the first scripts were finished I asked my colleague, Denis Moriarty, to join us with the special task of producing our location dialogue, and for the next four months preparations continued. Kenneth Dover translated most of the Greek texts we intended to use, and I continued to work on the scripts, adding and cutting, and deciding how I was going to direct the documentary scenes and the dramatised sequences.

At last we were ready to start. With Henry Farrar and our film crew we began shooting in Florence. Then we travelled to Rome and Paestum and crossed the Straits of Messina to Sicily. After we had filmed for several days in Syracuse, one of the most important Greek cities in the ancient world, Kenneth Dover joined us and we began to shoot the dialogue scenes. While I directed these, and Denis Moriarty contributed his easygoing yet firm and shrewd observations on the way our filmed talk was developing, Kenneth Dover got into his stride and I had the very great pleasure of listening to him share, with clarity and enthusiasm, some of what his lifelong study of Greek thought and Greek ways have brought him.

In Greece itself we filmed with Kenneth Dover for three weeks, and then he returned to Oxford and the new term there. We carried on working in the countryside, in the museums and on the ancient sites. We flew round the peak of Mt Olympus (home of the Greek gods), and sailed to some of the Greek islands that speckle the Aegean Sea—Melos (where the Venus de Milo comes from), Sifnos, Delos (according to legend the birthplace of the god Apollo), Andros and Santorini. Then, after three months location filming we returned to London and I began casting the scenes from Aeschylus, Herodotos, Thucydides, Plato and the other writers we had chosen. We were joined by our drama cameraman, Sid Davies; our designer, Dacre Punt, supervised the building of his sets, and we filmed the drama scenes for the whole series.

Finally I began, with Dave King, our film editor, to cut the films. The editing took several months. It was a slow process with its own changing rhythm. The first assembly worked in a way, it made sense, but it had no life of its own. We cut and reshaped the films many times. I wrote and rewrote the commentary, changing its direction to make the most of our transpositions (we moved the nine-minute Athenian democratic debate, for example, from the first film to the second, and the whole twenty-five-minute *Oresteia* sequence from the second film to the third), and altered its tone and content as different and better ways of relating the elements began to become clear from the developing picture and sound tracks.

My friend Walter Todds made many helpful suggestions about music, and at last we had nearly finished. Kenneth Dover came to see and hear fine cuts of the four films, and made valuable comments.

He gave me the typescript of this book; and it gives me great pleasure that his deep and generous involvement in a series of BBC television films has drawn out of him the clearest, fairest, best introduction to the achievements of the ancient Greeks that I have ever read. It is a beginning that I am delighted to share in.

*Christopher Burstall*
London, 1980

# Preface

Those who are looking for a systematic and comprehensive account of Greek history, society, religion, literature and art will find some good books listed on page 138. They may then wish to put this book back on the shelf, for it is neither systematic nor comprehensive. It has taken shape during the making of a set of television programmes, and it says what I most wanted to say about the Greeks in the short time available. The link between each topic and the next is dictated by my own train of thought.

Scholarly books are full of doubts, reservations and exceptions, and it is necessary that they should be. In this book, by contrast, I have cut a lot of corners in the effort to be definite, clear and simple, even when the truth is complicated and disputable. All the same, I have not said anything that I do not believe to be true.

*Kenneth Dover*

Homer is quoted in the translations by Robert S. Fitzgerald (*Iliad*, New York 1974; *Odyssey*, London 1962). All other translations are my own.

I have consistently said (e.g.) 'the four-hundreds BC' instead of 'the fifth century BC'. On the whole, people find it clearer.

I have not been entirely consistent in my use of the terms 'Athenian' and 'Attic', which can be treated as synonymous. We normally say 'Attic dialect' but 'Athenian literature', 'Athenian ships' but 'Attic vases', and so on.

*Chronological Tables*

I

BC 2000 Ancestors of Greeks probably in Greece by now.
    1750 Peak of Minoan civilisation in Crete.
    1500 Peak of Mycenaean civilisation. Hittite Empire in Asia Minor.
    1250 Decline and eclipse of Mycenaean civilisation.
    1000 Greek colonisation of eastern coasts of Aegean.
    750 Beginning of Greek colonisation in Mediterranean and Black Sea.
    500 Threat of Persian Empire to Greece.
    250 Hellenistic kingdoms.
      1 Whole Eastern Mediterranean now part of Roman Empire.

AD 500 Roman Empire in West broken up; Roman Empire in East (Greek-speaking) survives.
    1500 Roman Empire in East now part of Turkish Empire.

II

BC 750 Geometric Pottery. Beginning of Greek colonisation in Mediterranean and Black Sea.
    700 Homer.
    650 Early lyric poets. Early sculpture.
    600 End of Assyria. Lydia powerful in western Asia Minor.
    550 Rise of Persian Empire.
    500 Persian invasion of Greece defeated.
    450 Great age of Attic tragedy. Parthenon. Herodotos.
    400 Peloponnesian War. Socrates. Thucydides. Aristophanes.
    350 Plato.
    300 Alexander the Great; end of the Persian Empire.

# CHAPTER ONE

# Greeks and Others

## Two Lots of Greeks

When you come to Athens by air in daylight, you look down on the ruins of one of the most famous buildings in the world: the Parthenon, standing on the Acropolis, the rocky hill in the heart of Athens. Next day, perhaps, you go to the National Museum in Athens, and the likelihood is that the very first things you look at there are golden necklaces, masks, jewellery and inlaid daggers excavated a century ago from the royal graves at Mycenae.

If you imagined that the austere marble grandeur of the Parthenon and the intricate opulence of the gold from Mycenae are simply two different aspects of the same civilisation, the products of two different arts practised at the same time, you would be going wrong right at the start. They actually represent two different civilisations a thousand years apart. A thousand years is a long time, longer than from the Norman Conquest to our own day, and whatever is said about 'the ancient Greeks' in sweeping general terms is going to be no more secure, no more immune to criticism and qualification and reconsideration, than what the future will say about 'the English'.

The Greeks, the people who came to call themselves *Hellēnes*, can be defined as the people who spoke the language we call 'Greek'. There were plenty of them in Greece soon after 2000 BC. Where they came from is a controversial question, but there's nothing unusual, let alone mysterious, about that; after all, everyone comes from somewhere else, if you go back far enough.

About 1600 BC fortified palaces were built at a number of places in Greece. The most famous of these sites is at Mycenae; for that reason the Greeks who built and inhabited them are nowadays called 'Mycenaeans', and their time the 'Mycenaean period'. Their ruling class was rich; their artists and craftsmen were skilful; and their administrative organisation was elaborate. They developed a system of writing, but they seem to have used it only for inventories and other administrative records.

There is a limit to what can be said about a past people to whose thoughts and feelings we have no direct access through literature, laws or private documents. From archaeological evidence we can discover what crops they grew or how they built houses, and we can draw plenty of inferences about their religious practices; but we cannot know what they were really *like*.

Mycenaean civilisation endured for the best part of four centuries. It faded out in the period 1200–1100 BC: not submerged under any cataclysmic invasion from outside, but shredded by turbulent movements of peoples within Greece, an endless series of wars, the destruction of the fortified palaces, and the replacement, in one locality after another, of rulers who valued the arts by rulers who did not. The Mycenaean writing-system survived in a modified form far away in Cyprus, but in Greece and the Aegean it was forgotten. Good building ceased; craftsmanship degenerated. In pottery, the history of which we can follow right through because it is abundant and its fabric does not decompose, decoration became crude and naïve.

Then, between 800 and 700 BC, the Greek world comes to life for us in a new form. We see it first, as we might expect, in decorated pottery, where design becomes sensitive, elegant and ambitious. The alphabet is invented by adaptation of the writing-system used in Syria, and from then on literature is transmitted in writing. The 'real' Greeks, who have been with us ever since, have come into view, the Greeks whose civilisation generated great sculpture, drama, democracy and philosophy.

So, two lots of Greeks, separated by a trough of four centuries; and the link between them is Homer.

Homer was regarded by the Greeks as the supreme composer of epics, long narrative poems. Two such poems, the *Iliad* and the *Odyssey*, came to be treated as belonging in a class by themselves, and they are the only two (out of many) which have survived. Where and when Homer himself lived is a question about which the Greeks themselves disagreed so much that it is obvious they never had any good evidence; but for various reasons it is hard to push him back much beyond 700 BC, and his true date may be a bit later. His poetry was not about events of his own time, but about great men and wars of a remote age: above all, about the alliance of the states of the southern mainland of Greece, led by Agamemnon, king of Mycenae, against the city of Troy, on the Asiatic side of the Aegean.

Politically and geographically, the Greece of the *Iliad* is much more like Mycenaean Greece than anything that existed in Homer's own time. Many centres of power and wealth in Mycenaean Greece, such as Pylos and Mycenae itself, are important in Homer's poetry, but they had become negligible long before Homer. From about 1000 BC there were many Greek cities on the Asiatic coast of the Aegean, but in the world that Homer portrays that area is Greekless. In the *Iliad* Agamemnon's army and the Trojans fight with weapons of bronze, as the Mycenaeans did, but Homer's contemporaries fought with iron. In other words, the framework of the story which Homer tells is a very old one, and so are some of the details; but a great deal else in it belongs much later than the Mycenaeans.

When Schliemann excavated Mycenae a hundred years ago and found rich royal graves, he thought he was proving Homer's story true. Finding a gold mask in one grave, he was convinced he had 'looked upon the face of Agamemnon'. Unfortunately, the dates don't work out. Thanks to widespread systematic excavation of Mycenaean sites and the discovery of many links between Mycenaean artefacts and the cultures of the ancient Near East, we know immeasurably more about the Mycenaean period than Schliemann could know, and no one would now feel any confidence in putting a name to the man upon whose mask Schliemann gazed. It belongs to about 1550 BC. Now, the Greeks themselves made different estimates of the date of the Trojan War, but their most favoured pointed to the neighbourhood of 1200 BC. Excavation of Troy indicates that *somebody* burned it about that time, though of course the remains of a burned city don't tell us *who* burned it. The Greek estimates were based on the genealogies of noble families who claimed descent from Agamemnon or other heroes. We have some of these genealogies, and we can see for ourselves that (for what it is worth) they imply a date for the Trojan War in the period 1200–1100 BC, certainly not earlier.

Maybe there once lived eminent Greeks bearing the names of Homer's heroes – Agamemnon, Achilles, Odysseus and so on. Maybe they belonged to the time when Troy was destroyed. But in all human cultures tradition and legend so often run together famous names and famous events from quite different periods that Agamemnon or any other of Homer's heroes could as well belong to a time later than the Trojan War or much earlier. Homer links the first lot of Greeks to the second in the sense that he reveals to us the picture of the first lot which was entertained by the second. It was a picture of a rich, adventurous past, a heroic age, and down to the end of pagan Greek civilisation it furnished the staple material of serious poetry and drama.

### The Barbarian Context

Greece in ancient times was never a nation; it never had a capital, a government or a single ruling element. The typical Greek-speaking sovereign state was a tribe cultivating an area of land separated from the next cultivable area by a range of rocky hills or mountains. Somewhere on its land it created or inherited a concentration of buildings, surrounded by a defensive wall and, if possible, clustered round a fortified hill. There were hundreds of communities of this kind in Greece, many of them no larger than Kirriemuir or Lambourne, but each one a sovereign state making its own laws and very commonly in a state of war with one of its neighbours.

Nothing brings this home to us more vividly than standing on the citadel of Mycenae, on a day that is not too hot and hazy, and looking southwards. Only seven miles away the rocky citadel of Argos soars up from the plain. Look a little to the left, and you see the flat top of the fortifications of Tiryns, only ten miles away. For centuries these three places were independent sovereign states; but they are closer together than, say, Aylesbury, Berkhamsted and Leighton Buzzard.

'City' and 'city-state' may seem misleading ways of translating the Greek term (*polis*) for the independent sovereign community, because so few of those communities had a concentration of population of a size that we would nowadays call a 'city', but it would be more troublesome to use one word for big sovereign communities, another for small ones, and argue over what we should call the middle-sized.

What the Greek cities had in common was their language and the community of culture which followed from community of language: inter-state festivals of which religion, art and athletics were ingredients; temples and sanctuaries respected by all; free movement of artists and poets; the easy dissemination of ideas. People were thought of as Greeks if their native language was Greek, and not otherwise. Those whose native language was not Greek were called *barbaroi*, 'barbarians'. This became a derogatory word (and has remained so) when the Greeks acquired the firm conviction that their own culture and way of life were much better than anybody else's; but that conviction took a long time to grow.

It would be very surprising if it had *not* taken a long time; for whatever the achievements of the Greeks, they certainly did not create ancient civilisation, and as comparatively late arrivals on the ancient scene they did not lack respect for what they found already there. Karl Marx, a lifelong devotee of the Classics, once wrote about the Greeks: 'Why shouldn't the childhood of human society – the stage at which it attained its most attractive development – exercise an eternal charm, as an age that will never return?'[1] In 1857, when he wrote those words, good progress had been made for some time with the decipherment of Egyptian hieroglyphic inscriptions and papyri, and the decisive steps in the decipherment of Babylonian inscriptions had just been taken, but when people thought of 'the ancient world' they had in mind the Greeks, Romans and Hebrews, not the Egyptians and Babylonians. Nowadays it would seem odd to assign Socrates and the Parthenon to 'the childhood of human society'. Seen against a background of the whole history of human-like creatures living in groups and using tools, fire, colour and language, Socrates was

around only yesterday; he is virtually our contemporary. Placed in the
context of the history of the eastern Mediterranean and the Near East,
he stands no nearer to the beginnings of civilisation than he does to us.
Two and a half thousand years before Socrates was born the inhabitants
of ancient Egypt and of Mesopotamia (modern Iraq) had evolved systems
of writing and the distinctive styles of art, work and life which generated
ancient civilisation.

A summary description or tabulated chart of the history of the ancient
world down to the time of the Greeks can be cast either in terms of culture
and its diffusion or in terms of power and wealth. Part of the time,
especially in the first thousand years, it makes little difference, but it
makes quite a difference later. A table displaying rise, peak and decline
in terms of virtue and wisdom is, I fear, impracticable.

Let's take the first thousand years for granted and begin at 2000 BC.
At that time Egypt was one of the two great centres of power, wealth
and culture; the other was Mesopotamia. Mesopotamia is rather complicated: two quite different languages were spoken there, Sumerian and
Akkadian, the latter a 'Semitic' language (related to Hebrew and Arabic)
and destined gradually to replace Sumerian. Mesopotamia was, moreover, still a region of city-states; the unified kingdoms of 'Babylonia' and
'Assyria' had not yet taken shape. Greece and the Aegean are off the edge
of the world dominated by Egypt and Mesopotamia, but not in cultural
darkness: on the island of Crete the Minoans, builders of the great
palaces at Knossos and elsewhere, were developing a sophisticated and
quite distinctive culture of their own.

Now come down half a millennium, to the time of Mycenae at its
richest. There is a third centre of power and wealth in Asia, the Hittite
Empire in what is now Turkey. Mycenaean civilisation has flourished
by assimilating the arts and techniques of the Minoans. Eventually it takes
over Crete. At the same time as Mycenaean civilisation begins to fade
out (and with it, necessarily, the Minoan component which it had taken
over), the Hittite Empire dissolves and is succeeded by a number of
smaller power-centres.

The period of four centuries which I have described as a 'trough' in
the history of the Greek world, a 'dark age', was not that in the Near
East. A great military power arose: the kingdom of Assyria, insatiable,
ruthless, resilient, ruled by frightful men who were great builders and
patrons of the arts and (a thing for which historians bless them) addicted
to the compilation of archives and the publication of garrulous inscriptions. The Assyrians reached the Mediterranean, intimidated Egypt and
inflicted great sufferings on (among many others) a small people in Palestine whose religion and literature were destined to matter much more
in human history than anything the Assyrian kings had ever done (though
no one knew that yet).

While the Assyrian lion rampaged in Asia, the Greek mice multiplied and spread. Early in the 'dark age' they migrated in force across the Aegean and established cities on the big offshore islands and in many coastal areas. In the 700s and 600s BC they planted cities in the northern Aegean, the Black Sea, Sicily and South Italy, and eastern Libya. These 'colonies', as they are usually called, were not such in the sense that they were administered by the cities that sent them out, but new and independent city-states. A mother-city often wished, and sometimes tried, to exercise control over its colonies, but usually failed; on occasion, mother-city and colony went to war against each other. The effect of the era of Greek colonisation, which slowed down after the middle of the 500s but never entirely stopped, was to make the Greek world a linguistic and cultural unity which was spatially discontinuous. The map on the front endpapers shows how the Greek cities were distributed in 500 BC. It also shows the enormous extent of something that came into existence entirely between 600 and 500 BC: the Persian Empire.

One of the strangest things, at first sight, about the centuries of Assyrian domination is the frequency of rebellion against Assyria. The consequences of unsuccessful rebellion were often horrible; yet the resilience and tenacity of Assyria in the face of difficulties was matched by the irrepressible optimism of other peoples in combining against her (*this* time, they always thought, their gods would favour them). In the end they turned out to be right. Babylonia, in alliance with the Medes, a people who lived in the north-west quarter of what is now Iran, succeeded in capturing and destroying Nineveh, and suddenly Assyrian power vanished for ever. The Medes were one part of a complex of peoples speaking Indo-European languages closely related to the ancient languages of northern India. The other part of the complex was the Persians, and it was the Persian king who became not only ruler of the whole complex but also, within the space of a single generation, the heir to *all* the monarchies of the Near East. Babylonia, Egypt, all the cities and lands of Syria and Asia Minor, collapsed under Persian attack. By 520 BC the Persian Empire was the greatest centralised power the world had yet seen.

This was the point of imminent confrontation between Greek and 'barbarian'. Not, of course, the first conflict; wherever a Greek settlement was planted, intermittent warfare with the local peoples was an accepted risk, and there were Greek disasters. Moreover, some of the Greek cities in the eastern Aegean had become subjects of the king of Lydia in the early 600s, and when Lydia was brought into the Persian Empire so were they. Part of the population of one city, Phokaia, migrated westwards rather than surrender to the Persians, and settled in Corsica. They didn't last long there, because they encountered the hostility of two enemies much more formidable than local tribes: the Etruscans of central Italy, and Carthage (the modern Tunis). The Greek world, fragmentary and discontinuous as it was, had come up against a barrier, in east and west alike, which was not just a limitation on further spreading but carried an implicit threat of subjugation by 'barbarians'.

### Prizes for Coming First

I mentioned in the last section a dozen ancient peoples, and a more detailed story would have mentioned a lot more: Elamites, Mitannians, Urartians, Phrygians.... So: why always the *Greeks*?

Not so long ago many teachers in western Europe told their pupils that Greek was a uniquely subtle and expressive language, Greek art a set of unsurpassable models and Greek philosophy the foundation of wisdom. Their acquaintance with other languages and other artistic and philosophical traditions was hardly sufficient to furnish them with good arguments in favour of these propositions, so they had to use bad arguments instead. With every day that passes there are more things apart from Greek to be interested in, and a wider variety of models available to the artist and writer; and even if the first step in philosophy was taken by the Greeks, a modern philosopher can still take the hundredth by starting from the ninety-ninth.

Most readers of Greek literature in translation discover that it has great merits. But more than English or French literature? So much more that we should read it instead? There cannot be many professional classicists today who would be so arrogant as to say, 'Yes, instead!' We are more likely to rest content with the observation that the ancient Greek world presents us with *one* interesting civilisation, *one* great literature, which will stand comparison with any others.

To many people 'ancient' is an off-putting word, because the world has changed so much in our time as to create an assumption that no ancient writer can ever be dealing with the same human experience. Make the contrary assumption before you read any Greek literature, and see how it works out. You may sometimes encounter observations which have been overlaid for a long time and needed to be made afresh. For example, I learn from the *Science Journal* of April 1968 that a series of experiments has demonstrated that the sight of a weapon can exacerbate aggressive feelings. This was expressed in a proverb, twice used by Homer: 'iron, of itself, draws a man after it'.

Different people have criticised classical education for different reasons. Thomas Hobbes wrote in 1651 that 'there was never any thing so dearly bought, as these western parts have bought the learning of the Greek and Latin tongues' — because Greek and Roman notions of 'liberty' encourage people, he thought, in impudent attempts to control their sovereign rulers.[2] Another eminent English philosopher, John Locke, writing in 1695, decried the teaching of Latin verse composition in school

7

on the grounds that it might encourage in a boy a vein of poetry disastrously incompatible with hard-headed money-making. Locke still thought that Latin was essential in the education of a *gentleman*.[3] Sentiments of that kind, coupled with the fact that it takes time and a lot of hard work to learn to read Greek and Latin fluently, have led to vilification of classical studies as 'élitist'. Well, I despise the use of thought-substitutes ending in -ism and -ist, but if Greek is élitist, that's one up to élitism.

A more serious hostility to classical studies is founded on the charge that Greek society is a bad model: slave-owning, contemptuous of women and addicted to war. A Black Power spokesman said:

> We are told that Western Civilisation begins with the Greeks, and the epitome of that is Alexander the Great. The only thing that I can remember about Alexander the Great was that at age twenty-six he wept because there were no other people to kill, murder and plunder. And that is the epitome of Western Civilisation.[4]

Greek society is certainly a bad model in some ways. So is every other known society, in some ways. I am more interested in the ways in which any given society is a good model.

A casual acquaintance with the ancient world suggests that there were a great many things which the Greeks did, said and thought for the very first time in human history. To sustain such a claim takes a lot more than casual acquaintance, because the assertion, for instance, that 'the Greeks were the *first* people to think that matter might be made of indestructible particles' implies '*No* Egyptian, Mesopotamian, Hittite, Israelite, Phoenician, etc., had *ever* thought that matter might be made of indestructible particles'. That proposition is one which, although it could be disproved by a single datum, could never conceivably be proved. By the time we had found it to be valid in respect of ancient oriental texts discovered so far, more texts would have been published; many more still, untranslated, even unread, would have piled up in museums; and new and controversial interpretations of some existing texts would have been put forward. In offering opinions on what the Greeks did for the first time, I can only do my best and hope that the reader will always understand phrases like 'So far as I know' and 'On the evidence up to date'. There is the further complication that many interesting things were done and said and thought in ancient times in China. I confess that I know nothing about ancient China. I know nothing about basketball or biochemistry, either, but that can't be helped; life is short, and even the joy of learning palls at times. Fortunately, since I am concerned with what happened down to 300 BC at the latest, and to a great extent with what happened before 500 BC, I risk very little by saying boldly that the Greeks and the Near East were part of *our* history, and ancient China was not; nor, for all practical purposes, was ancient India. So, when I say 'the first time' I shall mean 'the first time in *our* history'.

We have already seen that the Greeks did not exist in a vacuum. Their civilisation took shape at a certain time and place, in a long-established context. Anything we say about them may turn out to be true of their entire context as well, or it may be true of them alone; without looking to see, we cannot know in advance which will turn out to be the case.

Obviously, if we browse through the literature and the documents of the ancient Eastern civilisations, we shall constantly be struck by reminders of the Greeks. Many of the things we notice will turn out to be ideas and practices shared by the Greeks not simply with their fore-runners but also with any number of other cultures, past and present, and curious to us only because our own technological culture is so different from everything, everywhere, that has gone before. For example, a Hittite inscription which gives the wording of a very elaborate oath of loyalty taken by soldiers includes many passages of the following kind:

> Then he places wax and mutton fat in their hands. He throws these on a flame and says, 'Just as this wax melts, and just as the mutton fat dissolves — whoever breaks these oaths and shows disrespect to the king of the Hatti land, let him melt like wax, let him dissolve like mutton fat.' The men declare, 'So be it!'[5]

Seven hundred years later Homer describes the making of a truce between the Greeks and the Trojans. A truce requires an oath, so they sacrifice two lambs and pour a libation of wine to the gods.

> And men said among the Greeks and Trojans, 'Zeus, mightiest and most glorious, and all the immortal gods – whichever side first violates the oath, may their brains flow upon the ground just as this wine flows, their brains and their children's, and may their wives become the spoil of others!'[6]

Not only religious practices but ingredients of myths and poetic motifs surface in two or more ancient civilisations, sometimes over long periods of time. What we are looking for is things which surface for the very first time in Greek civilisation; and preferably things of real importance or, if trivial, at least carrying important implications. We shall not, if we are prudent, spend too long seeking these things in mathematics and applied science; until comparatively recently, the achievements of the Greeks in those fields have been somewhat overrated and those of the older Eastern civilisations underrated. True, the Greeks did invent the alphabet, and this very simple system of twenty-four signs meant that far more people could read and write in the Greek world than in Egypt or Mesopotamia, which used writing-systems of subtle beauty but horrible complexity. But the Greek set of signs was taken from Syria, at some time well before 700 BC, and the inhabitants of Syria and Palestine had for a long time used a simple system whose only drawback was that it left out short vowels. The Greeks remedied that by using for vowels some of the signs they did not need for consonants, an essential step if the system was to be practicable for Greek, but by no means the most inventive step, which was the substitution of simplicity for complexity.

In the arts, it is open to us to prefer Greek epic poetry to Mesopotamian, or Greek lyric and dramatic poetry to Egyptian, and open to us to wonder whether Egyptian oratory, though an art-form developed for discriminating audiences, was really as subtle as Greek. These are matters of more and less, not of total Greek innovation. The speed and exuberance of Greek experiment in the visual arts come in a different category; I shall revert to them in chapters 3 and 4. Experiment is even more conspicuous in the organisation of society and the exercise of the intellect.

Democracy was certainly Greek. Shaky and partial, but still recognisably a major step towards equality under the law and the participation of people in the taking of decisions which affected their lives. Democracy was not, of course, designed by a committee round a table. It was a product of Greek behaviour, for the unruly Greek tribes did not bring with them into Greece the habit of throwing themselves on their faces before a ruler or addressing him in the formulae of adulation. The world portrayed by Homer is a world ruled by kings, but one of its remarkable features is the freedom with which lesser men speak their minds to greater men; they risk anger, abuse and violence, but the risk has more in common with prodding a bull than with ridiculing the sacraments. Democracy was a logical consequence of irreverence.

When the Greeks borrowed arts and techniques from their venerable Eastern neighbours, they showed no inclination to invest their big men with the frightening aura of divinity which belonged to the Egyptian and Mesopotamian kings. That servility was not in fact a universal characteristic of ancient man, but a special development, slow in growth, of centralised monarchies. It may well be that if we go further back in time, to the early cities of Mesopotamia, we find something more like the Greek city-states. Seventeen centuries before Homer, two thousand years before Plato, a Mesopotamian king, Urukagina of Lagash, boasted of how he had reformed age-old abuses, ended unjust oppression and 'restored freedom' to the people of his city. The Sumerian word translated 'freedom', *amargi*, is plainly a good thing, of which one boasts, and some five centuries later another Mesopotamian legislator is praised for 'procuring the *amargi* of the sons and daughters of Ur...., upon whom servitude had been imposed'. I understand that Urukagina's document is the earliest surviving text in the world containing a word which we can translate as 'freedom'.[7] But there are many different freedoms. *Amargi*, like the Akkadian word which translates it in bilingual documents, covers manumission of slaves, remission of debts and immunity from taxation. If we were to say that the Sumerians instituted the practice of free speech between free men, we would need to ask first, 'Did *amargi* include free-dom to criticise the ruler who conferred *amargi*?'; and unless we could see reason to think that it did, we should go on regarding Greek civilisa-tion as the first of the ancient civilisations in which it was common for people to insist on speaking their minds.

If the man in the street speaks his mind on issues of practical politics, the intellectual speaks his mind on history, tradition, religion and science. We shall find, I think, that the distinctive new feature of Greek civilisa-tion is the readiness of the Greek to dissociate himself from established ideas, to speculate, to use his imagination, to say, 'This is what *I* think; and I this is why I think it . . .', and (what matters most) to say it without fear of monarch, noble, priest, gang or mob. Without *too* much fear, that is; these things are relative. And the reluctance of the ancient oriental to express sceptical reservations is not absolute either. Here are a few instances of what I would call Greek attitudes expressed long before the Greeks. First, from an ancient Egyptian story, *King Cheops and the Magicians*:

> The king's son Hardedef rose to speak, and he said, 'You have heard examples of the skill of those who have passed away, but there one cannot know truth from falsehood. But there is with Your Majesty, in your own time, one who is not known to you. . . .'[8]

Secondly, from an Egyptian song:

> Now, I have heard the sayings
> of Iyemhotep and Hardedef,
> which are quoted
> in the proverbs so much.
>
> What are their cult places?
> Their walls are dismantled,
> and their cult places exist no more,
> as if they had never been.
>
> There is no one who can return from there
> to describe their nature, to describe their dissolution,
> that he may still our desires,
> until we reach the place where they have gone.
>
> So may your desire be fulfilled:
> allow the heart to forget
> the performance of services for you.
> Follow your desire while you live.[9]

And an excerpt from regulations for a Hittite temple:

> If an ox or a sheep is driven up to the god as food, and you appropriate for yourselves either a fattened ox or a fattened sheep and substitute a lean one which you have slaughtered . . . and speak as follows, 'Since

he is a god, he will not say anything, and will not do anything to us'
– just think how the man reacts who sees his morsel snatched away from
before his eyes! The will of the god is strong. It does not make haste
to seize, but when it seizes it does not let go again.[10]

Not everyone, perhaps, will agree that Greek scepticism and independence of judgement are the most important strand in the history of the
West, even if they are taken (and not everyone, in any case, would so
take them) to be the moving force of Greek artistic and literary innovation. Some will give pride of place to the idea of a single righteous God,
the distinctive contribution of the Jews. There is a point beyond which
it is hard to argue about degrees of importance.

And suppose we decide that the most important things in the history
of our civilisation were first done by the Greeks, what do we do about
it? Give them a prize, pat them on the head, and send them off to have
a nice tea? The value of what is done does not depend on who first did
it, and a historian can fairly criticise the compilation of a list of 'firsts'
as historically trivial, suitable only for inclusion in a Book of Records.
But if all Greek innovations proceeded ultimately from one fundamental
revolution in attitude, and if that revolution is one from which we can
learn and profit directly, the case is altered. One argument of this book
is that they *did* all proceed from one fundamental revolution, and that
we *can* learn and profit directly from the Greek example.

### A Persian Frontier Problem[11]

Darius 'the Great King, King of Kings, King of the World'
became ruler of the Persian Empire in 521 BC 'by the favour and gift of the
Wise God'. He was not the son of his predecessor, but the choice of an
aristocratic conspiracy which ended a turbulent episode, and the first year
of his reign was passed in the suppression of revolts. He showed himself
as quick and efficient a conqueror as the Assyrian kings before him, and
he adopted their style too:

> ... Fravartish was seized and led to me. I cut off his nose and ears and
> tongue and put out one of his eyes. He was kept bound at the entrance
> to my palace; all the people saw him. Afterwards I impaled him at Ecba-
> tana; and the men who were his chief followers, those at Ecbatana within
> the fortress, I hung out [i.e. flayed them and displayed their skins] ...[12]

The water which separated Asia from Europe marked at that time the
edge of Darius' world. The Greek cities on the Aegean coast of Asia were
on that edge, and over the edge were the Aegean islands and the mainland
of Greece. A ruler who has every reason to think he controls the only
great power in the world does not like untidy bits of independence lying
around, and Darius did not leave Europe undisturbed for long. Interven-

ing in the big Greek islands which lay closest to the Asiatic shore, he brought them under his control. With their help, he invaded Europe, crossed the Danube, and campaigned deep into the plains of eastern Romania, towards the Ukraine. This was not a profitable adventure for him, but Persian power was more enduringly established along the north coast of the Aegean.

Whether – or how soon – Darius intended to invade Greece itself is not known, because some of his Greek subjects in Asia, the 'Ionian' cities, combined to rebel. It took the Persians five years to extinguish this rebellion completely, but its prospects had never been good. The rebellious Greeks had sought help from the Greek mainland, but had got little. Two cities, however, Athens and Eretria, sent contingents in time for the rebels' most showy achievement, a march inland to capture the city of Sardis. Herodotos, who wrote the history of the conflict between Greeks and Persians, tells a memorable anecdote about the consequences:

> When King Darius heard the news that the city of Sardis had been taken and burnt by the Athenians and Ionians, it is said that he did not worry at all about the Ionians, for he well knew that they would pay dearly for their rebellion, but he asked, 'Who are the Athenians?' On being told, he demanded his bow; he took it up and put an arrow on the string and shot it up towards the sky, saying, as he let fly the shaft, 'Lord of the Gods, may it come to pass that I revenge myself on the Athenians!' Then he commanded one of his servants to say three times every day, at the hour of dinner, 'Master, remember the Athenians!'[13]

A few years passed, and in 490 BC Darius sent a punitive 'frontier' expedition by sea against Athens and Eretria. The Persians devastated Eretria, but when they landed at Marathon, on the east coast of Attica, the Athenians repelled them and drove them to re-embark. Marathon ever after was a proud name in Athenian tradition; the very first alien attempt on the mainland of Greece had been defeated by Athens virtually alone, helped only by the men of the little city of Plataea.

Darius died before he could prepare an expedition on a grander scale, and it fell to his son Xerxes to organise a great army and fleet designed to subjugate the whole of the Greek mainland for good. This army, led by Xerxes himself, entered the northern regions of Greece in the summer of 480 BC, the fleet keeping pace offshore. Army and fleet alike were on a scale quite outside Greek experience, and the tradition which Herodotos inherited and consolidated spoke of millions of men and thousands of ships. We don't have to believe that, but we do have to remember that the Persian king was, for all practical purposes, perceived as ruler of the world, and when his forces flooded on southwards the cities of northern and central Greece submitted without a fight. Further south, the temper was different. Most Peloponnesian cities, dominated by Sparta, were determined to resist; and outside the Peloponnese so was Athens.

When it was known that the Persian invasion was imminent, the Athenians sent emissaries to the oracle of Apollo at Delphi, to ask the god, 'What shall we do?' It was normal for a city-state faced with a difficult decision to consult an oracle, and by this time Delphi had unique prestige as an oracle in mainland Greece. Of course, there was no compulsion on the god to answer a question, and when he did answer, it was possible to misinterpret his words disastrously. But oracles were not simply a piece of machinery; they were manifestations of the graciousness of the gods, and *any* hint about the future, no matter how fragmentary or ambiguous, was a precious gleam in the darkness of human ignorance. When the Athenian emissaries asked how they should act in face of the Persian threat, they were aghast at the answer: the god told them to 'flee to the ends of the earth'. Being Greeks, they were not all inclined to say 'Thy will be done'. They threatened instead that unless they were given a better answer they would starve themselves in the sanctuary and defile it by dying there. So the god had second thoughts, and offered an enigmatic hope by telling them to trust in their 'wooden walls'. This answer they took back to Athens.

In the years since Marathon the Athenians had built up a big fleet of warships and trained themselves to use it. Realising that these ships were their 'wooden walls', they abandoned their city and their land and moved their entire population across to the offshore island of Salamis – all except a foolish minority who entrenched themselves behind a wooden wall on the Acropolis, expecting divine aid, and were quickly disposed of by the invaders. At Salamis the Athenian fleet was united with the other Greek fleets. There was much bitter argument; they were not accustomed to co-operating. The Peloponnesians hankered after a fixed defence, a fortified line across the narrowest part of the isthmus that joins the Peloponnese to the rest of the mainland. The Athenians saw plainly that so long as the Persian fleet was undefeated, any fortification on land could be turned. It was therefore imperative to fight a sea-battle *now*. Themistokles, one of the Athenian commanders, saw to it that the Persian king got a message, which purported to be friendly, telling him that the Greek fleet was in disarray and on the point of dispersing. This was meant to tempt the king to send his fleet into the narrow waters between Salamis and the mainland for an easy 'dawn round-up'. This he did, and his fleet went in to meet disaster head-on.

Eight years after the battle the tragic poet Aeschylus produced his *Persians*, in which the scene is set at the Persian court and Xerxes' mother, the dowager queen, hears the terrible news of Salamis from a messenger. Here is part of the messenger's speech:

> When the white horses of the day spread brightness
> on all the earth, from the Greek side we heard

the ringing voice of [*incredulously*] music, fervent song!
The echo from the cliffs of Salamis
threw back a shrill reply.
And fear ran through us all, the host of Asia;
for now we knew we had deceived ourselves.
That solemn song was not the sound of fear,
but heart and courage moving into battle.
A trumpet-cry set land and sea afire.
Straightway their oars struck in the sea together,
rhythmic, steady, cleaving the salt foam.
Suddenly they were all before our eyes.
Their right wing led, ordered and sure and fast;
behind it, all their fleet raced to attack,
and we could hear the chorus of their cry:
'Go, sons of Greeks! Set free your fatherland,
your wives, your children, temples of your gods,
ancestral tombs! Now – all is at stake!'
On our side a roar of Persian tongue
replied; this was the moment for the fight.
At once the iron ram struck, ship into ship;
the first to ram was Greek, tearing away
the high stern of a warship from Phoenicia;
a second Greek drove at another victim.
At first the great stream of the Persian fleet
held out; but when the ships were massed together,
tightly in turmoil, none could help another –
ship tearing sister-ship with teeth of iron,
shearing away the oars – while all around
the Greek fleet circled, cool and sharp, and struck.
Ships were capsized; the waves could not be seen,
smothered in shattered wrecks and human flesh.
On shores and rocks dead men were crowded thick.
From end to end, in all the fleet of Asia,
the rowers turned to panic and retreat.
But *they*, with splintered oars and bits of plank,
were hacking, chopping.
We were a catch of tunny in their net.
So all the sea was filled with cries and groans
till the dark eyes of night were closed upon it.[14]

Aeschylus had fought at Marathon, and he fought at Salamis too –
probably not as a sailor on a warship, but as a soldier posted on the
shore, waiting to kill enemy sailors who struggled out of the water. He
was one of the pioneers of the theatre, perhaps the most important single
figure in the history of European drama. There exists an epitaph on him,
which he is said to have composed for himself, and it reflects the priorities
of his time: it tells us that he fought against the Persians, but does not

mention that he wrote plays as well. The striking feature of his *Persians* is its dignity. He might have made the Persians ridiculous and contemptible, jabbering foreigners' Greek, wretched victims of innate Greek superiority. We know that he might have done, because two generations later another poet did. Aeschylus does not deny his Persians courage; he sees and expresses their suffering and despair as if he were a defeated Persian, not an exultant Greek; and he emphasises – through the ghost of Darius, who appears in answer to the invocations of the chorus and the queen – that the Greeks owed their victory not just to themselves, but to the good will of the gods. Xerxes had offended the gods by destroying sanctuaries in Greece, but above all he had provoked their malice by overreaching himself.

The idea that the gods slap down any mortal who becomes too powerful, rich and ambitious was widespread among the Greeks. Herodotos portrays a Persian noble as warning Xerxes, at the time when the invasion of Greece was first mooted:

> It is always the biggest buildings and the tallest trees that are struck by lightning. The gods are accustomed to throw down whatever rises too high.[15]

A bleak doctrine, perhaps, but easy to reconcile with what the Greeks saw happen. To the Athenian audience, seeing and hearing the homecoming of Xerxes in Aeschylus' *Persians*, the formalised co-ordination of despairing gestures and cries of lamentation portrayed human misfortune first and enemy misfortune second.

Xerxes in fact did not give up easily or all at once. When he returned to Asia, he left in central Greece an army of formidable size and quality, commanded by Mardonios. The Athenians and the Greeks of the Peloponnese had to reflect and decide afresh: surrender or – possibly, in the end, unsuccessful – resistance? In this context, 'resistance' meant destruction of Mardonios' army, if they could achieve that; nothing less would do. They decided that they must achieve it, and the last great battle of the Persian invasion was fought between some forty thousand heavy infantry of the allied Greek states (plus a very large number of light-armed soldiers) and a Persian army, including strong cavalry and contingents from northern and central Greece, which Greek tradition (perhaps mistakenly) believed to be four times as large. The battleground was the gently undulating ground by the city of Plataea, below Mount Kithairon – an archetypal battlefield, on which it is the easiest thing in the world to visualise glittering masses of troops advancing to the attack, and one of the hardest to work out, Herodotos' narrative in hand, *which* troops were *where* at *what* stage of the battle. The days that led up to the battle were full of uncertainties, frustrations and perils for the Greeks, but when it came to the hand-to-hand fighting the heavy armouring of the Greek infantryman was decisive. The Persian survivors retreated from Greece, and no Persian king ever tried to invade Greece again.

Few people, if any, outside Greece had believed that the Greeks could defeat Xerxes. Perhaps there were not many in Greece itself who believed it in those chill moments when reason insists on being heard. But now they had won after all; a conglomeration of little cities on the fringe of the world ruled by the King of Kings had humbled him. No wonder that from then on the Greeks thought themselves the best people in the world; as a rhetorical writer put it more than a century later, some felt that the Greeks were to the rest of the human race as human beings are to the rest of the animal kingdom (and the writer, being Athenian, added: as the Athenians are to other Greeks). It is interesting that they rarely thought of their superiority in terms of 'race' or genetic factors, and they attached no importance to differences of colour. Some of them theorised about the part played by climate, soil and water in determining apparent national differences of behaviour and temperament. What seemed to them most significant were laws, customs, way of life and language – all the alterable things about which a people can grow careless and put its own culture at risk.

The defeat of Xerxes marks the beginning of what we call the 'Classical' period and the end of the 'Archaic' period. What is best known about the Greeks nowadays is Classical: drama, the Parthenon sculptures, Socrates, the greatest works of history, philosophy and oratory. It may be tempting to think that the sudden consciousness of superiority inspired by the defeat of Xerxes was a *cause* of these extraordinary achievements. But this temptation is quashed by the evidence, for *all* the distinctive features of Greek culture – artistic experiment, free-ranging speculation, drama, democratic assemblies – had plainly taken shape *before* the Persian invasion. Refusal to accept defeat before putting the need for acceptance to the test was itself a manifestation, an effect, of a way of life which evolved during the Archaic period, a way of life which had something new and remarkable to offer.

### The Fate of the City

Collaboration was required for the defeat of the Persian invasion: above all, between Athens, which provided the bulk of the fleet at Salamis, and Sparta, which provided the supreme command and the hard core of the army at Plataea. This was a very unusual degree of collaboration, and it was not destined to last. Faced with a threat so close and terrible that it cannot be talked away, people get together. When the threat recedes, they revert to their traditional ways of doing things. The Greek tradition is acutely summed up by a speaker in Plato's *Laws* in the middle of the 300s BC:

> What most people call 'peace' is only a name. In reality every city is always in a state of undeclared war against every other city.[16]

We have already had a look across at Argos and Tiryns from the citadel of Mycenae, and we have to remind ourselves that at the time of the Persian invasion these three places were independent sovereign states, and had been for centuries. Soon after the defeat of the Persians, Argos turned upon Tiryns and Mycenae and swallowed them up, absorbing the population into her own and abandoning the sites. This nicely illustrates the most important of the restraints on Greek fragmentation: obliteration of the smallest and weakest by more powerful neighbours.

Much more commonly, the independence of a weak city-state was to some degree diminished – to a degree varying very greatly from time to time and place to place – by subordination to a stronger city. Subordination was usually called 'alliance'. A weak city allied to a strong might well have its own constitution, legal code and coinage, and it talked the language of sovereign independence; but it was unlikely to be a democracy if its stronger ally was not, it was often expected to contribute its forces to an expedition on demand, and it might be subject to a demand for regular tribute. In the years after the Persian war, Greece and the Aegean, ostensibly a vast swarm of city-states, were in fact largely polarised between two powerful cities, Athens and Sparta. 'The Athenians and their allies' was the formal designation of what we commonly call 'the Athenian Empire', comprising the islands and the northern and eastern coasts of the Aegean, paying annual tribute to Athens and subject, as the 400s went on, to an increasing degree of political and administrative control by Athens. 'The Spartans and their allies', or 'the Peloponnesians', or 'the Peloponnesian League', are more elusive entities, but the reality behind them is that Sparta was indisputably the strongest military power on land, dominated most of the Peloponnese, and had some allies outside the Peloponnese as well.

The greatest collision between Athens and Sparta, the 'Peloponnesian War' (we name it from an Athenian standpoint), lasted from 431 to 404 BC, with a few years of uneasy truce round about half-time. It ended with the total defeat and capitulation of Athens and the dissolution of her control over her 'empire'. It looked as if it had changed the balance of power in Greece for ever; and in a sense it did, but by substituting a complicated and shifting balance for a simple one.

Let us again try to translate the situation into visual terms by going on to another high place and looking at the view – this time Acrocorinth, the 1800-foot mountain which was the fortified citadel of ancient Corinth. From the top of Acrocorinth we can see south-westwards into the territory of Argos and the mountains of Arcadia, and to the east the Acropolis of Athens could once be seen (nowadays lurid industrial haze intervenes);

north-westwards, we look far into central Greece and may glimpse moun-
tain-tops seventy miles away. Corinth is literally in the middle of things,
just where the Peloponnese hangs by a thread from the rest of the mainland. Politically, too, Corinth was in the middle of things. In the Peloponnesian War she was an ally of Sparta, and remained so to the end of
the war despite a period of indignant estrangement in the middle. Yet
within ten years we find a new alignment: victorious Sparta has aroused
resentment, and Corinth and Thebes are in alliance with their former
enemy Athens against her. The first part of the 300s is marked by the
rise of Thebes as the chief military power on the mainland and the deposi-
tion of Sparta from that eminence. Xenophon, whose history of this period
survives, ends his narrative on a sombre note after describing the battle
of Mantinea (362 BC):

> Each side said it had won; but neither was demonstrably any better off,
> in territory, city or power, than before the battle was fought. After the
> battle confusion was greater in Greece, and decisive outcome further
> away, than previously.
>
> This is the point at which I propose to end. Someone else will perhaps
> concern himself with subsequent events.[17]

At the time Xenophon wrote those words, a 'decisive outcome' was
surprisingly near at hand, but it was not one achieved by the Greeks themselves. Far away beyond the northern horizon lay the kingdom of Macedon, the region where nowadays Greece, Yugoslavia and Bulgaria meet.
The kings of Macedon claimed Greek heroic ancestry, and from the 400s
they sometimes offered lavish patronage to distinguished Greek poets
(Euripides, for example). To judge from what little we know of the Macedonian language, it was very close to Greek, but not close enough for
the people who spoke it to be welcomed as members of the Greek linguistic
community. They were regarded as a primitive, ill-organised and unreli-
able people. When Philip II became king of Macedon in 359 BC, it was
a little while before the Greeks realised that his intelligence, energy and
ruthlessness were very quickly transforming Macedon into a military
power quite unlike the Macedon to which they had long been accustomed. The Athenian politician Demosthenes, indignant at Athens'
failure to defend her possessions and allies in the north Aegean against
Philip's aggression, exclaims:

> And he's so far from being a Greek or having the remotest connection
> with us Greeks that he doesn't even come from a country with a name
> that's respected. He's a lousy *Macedonian* – and not so long ago you
> couldn't even buy a decent *slave* from Macedon.[18]

Less than twenty years after his accession to the throne of Macedon
– a period in which he had established his power in Greece partly by

his military speed and efficiency, partly by exploiting the mutual resentments of Greek city-states – Philip resoundingly defeated the last and biggest combination of states to stand against him. Then he summoned a congress at Corinth (in the middle of things, as usual) and constituted them a league of allies. Two hunks of stone in the Epigraphical Museum at Athens, looking rather like small boulders, are pieces of

These two pieces of stone are part of the Athenian copy of the treaty which made Philip II of Macedon the overlord of Greece.

the official Athenian copy of the 'foundation-document' of this league. The lettering is small and badly worn, but we can read at the beginning some words of the oath which the delegates swore, and where words are lost our knowledge of the formulae of similar documents makes it possible to fill in the gaps:

> I swear by Zeus, Earth, Sun, Poseidon, Athena, Ares and all gods and goddesses that I will abide by the peace and I will not break the treaty made with Philip the Macedonian. Nor will I bear arms by land or sea against any who abide by this oath. . . . And if anyone acts in contravention of the treaty, I will intervene as demanded by those who are wronged, and I will make war on violators of the General Peace in accordance with the decisions of the General Council and the demands of the head of the Alliance . . .[19]

The head of the Alliance (literally 'Leader') was Philip, and the effect of the oath was to ensure that it should be Macedon, in the long run, which decided what was to happen in Greece and the Aegean.

Two years later Philip was murdered by one of his own men, at a time when he was planning an attack on the (by now rather ramshackle) Persian Empire. His youthful son Alexander, 'the Great', carried out this plan in spectacular fashion, conquering in a few years everything from Libya to Samarkand and Karachi. When he died in Babylon at the age of thirty-two his generals carved up the vast empire he had conquered. From then on the history of the distribution of power in the Greek world is a history of monarchies rather than city-states. But 'the Greek world' was much bigger than it had been, for Alexander's conquests had spread the Greek language and Greek culture all over the Near East, and the rulers everywhere were Macedonians and Greeks. Egypt, for example, was ruled by a Greek-speaking dynasty for the next three hundred years, and Greek settlement there was extensively superimposed on the native Egyptian population.

Just at the time of this explosive diffusion of Greek from the eastern end of the Mediterranean, the remoter future was taking shape in the central Mediterranean. The city of Rome was extending its control over Italy. A hundred years later the Romans were in Spain, Sicily and the Balkans. The history of Roman relations with Macedonian kings and Greek cities and leagues of cities is complicated. It ceased to be so in 146 BC, when the Romans burnt, sacked and obliterated the city of Corinth. This terrifying lesson was never forgotten; from then on Greece was a peaceful province of the Roman Empire. Greek was the official language of the eastern half of that Empire, Latin the official language of the western half.

The Greeks and the Romans had a good deal in common. Both peoples had traditions rooted in the idea of the citizen-assembly, hostile to monarchy and to servility. Their religions were alike enough for most of their deities to be readily identified – Greek Zeus with Roman Jupiter, Greek Hera with Roman Juno, and so on – and their myths to be fused. Their languages worked in similar ways, and were ultimately related, both being members of the Indo-European language-family which stretches from Bangladesh to Iceland. The Latin alphabet (that is, our own alphabet) was derived directly from a form of the Greek alphabet used by Greek colonies in part of southern Italy.

But there was one great difference between Greeks and Romans. Rome, one single city – just as Athens or Sparta was a single city – progressed relentlessly over the centuries to create the Roman Empire, embracing the entire Mediterranean basin, together with Britain and parts of central Europe. The Roman Empire was eventually able to experience a 'decline and fall' (having lasted twice as long as the British Empire) because it attained a position of supremacy from which decline was possible. The 'Greek Empire' could not decline, because no such thing as a Greek Empire ever existed, unless we count the brief moment for which Alexander of Macedon ruled over the vast area he had conquered. (When the Roman Empire in the western Mediterranean broke up, the eastern half, with its capital at Constantinople, lasted until it was destroyed by the Turks in the fifteenth century, but the Greek-speaking people of Constantinople called themselves 'Romans'.)

Rome did not doubt that she was an instrument of Providence, destined to rule for ever, and that the Greeks were among the many unfortunate peoples from whom Providence had turned away her face. Torn as they were by civil war for much of their history, the Romans none the less derived an extraordinary confidence from the systematic, meticulous organisation of their own military and administrative activities, and their confidence is reflected in the uniformity with which they put their system smoothly and quickly into effect, wherever in the world they went.

But every Roman knew that the Greeks enjoyed an artistic and intellectual inheritance much older and immeasurably richer than his own. With few exceptions, he respected this inheritance and assimilated it for the artistic enrichment of his own culture. 'Captive Greece', said the poet Horace, 'took her rude conqueror captive.' If a Roman asked himself what kind of plays his ancestors were writing when Aeschylus was alive at Athens, he knew that the answer was: none whatsoever. Writing good poetry is, of course, only one out of a very large range of possible human activities, and different civilisations have different priorities. The Roman's respect for Greek culture sometimes had a rather patronising colouring; it reminds us of the expression into which a self-made millionaire thinks it appropriate to compose his features when he has occasion to speak of the Church of England, medieval archaeology or a distinguished violinist.

Later ages too, in studying the past, can have various priorities. This must be at least the hundredth book about the Greeks published for the general reader in the English-speaking world during the last thirty years; how many have there been about the Romans?

# CHAPTER TWO

# A View from Syracuse

## The Sons of Deinomenes

For a very long time now most people's view of the ancient Greek world has been 'Athenocentric'. Athens was never, in ancient times, the 'capital' of Greece, for Greece was not a united country and had no capital. Politically, the city-state of Athens dominated only part of Greece, and only for a time. Yet most of the names of famous Greeks that come quickly to mind – Socrates, for example, or Plato, or Aeschylus – turn out to be names of Athenians; or again, the things we associate with the Greeks – tragedy, philosophy, democracy – are either Athenian innovations or things which attained their fullest development at Athens. The dominant position of Athens in our mental picture of the Greek world is a cultural dominance; it comes from the fact that the Athenians of the classical age had more to say than anyone else and created a great richness of literary forms in which to say it. It was their dialect which gave rise to the standard Greek of later times and the dialects of Greece today.

Yet if you had asked a Greek early in the 400s BC, 'Which is the biggest, richest, most powerful, most cultured city in the Greek world?', many a Greek would have answered, without hesitation, 'Syracuse'. Syracuse (*Surakousai* to the Greeks, *Siracusa* to the people who live there now) lies on the east coast of Sicily, and it was one of the very first 'colonies' to be planted in the central Mediterranean when the colonising movement began in the 700s BC. The Corinthians, who founded it, must for some time have had their eye on it as an ideal site: a wonderful harbour, three and a half kilometres at its widest, with an entrance just over one kilometre wide; a rocky island big enough for a Greek city, possessing an unfailing spring of water, and so close to the mainland that it could be joined to it by a causeway; abundance of fertile land on one side, and on the other a limestone plateau from which unlimited building stone could be quarried. Standing on the plateau today, able to look up and down the coast, we can just manage to see it in our mind's eye as the

Corinthians saw it; but it needs a very hard effort to think away the haze that hangs over the miles of oil refineries to the north.

The rise of Syracuse to a position of political and military dominance among the Greek cities founded in Sicily was a quick and dramatic development in the early 400s, and it happened, paradoxically, when a certain Gelon, ruler of the city of Gela, became master of Syracuse. Gelon transferred himself to Syracuse, brought half the population of Gela with him, tidied up the south-east corner of Sicily by destroying some smaller cities (with selective importation of their population too into Syracuse), and set about building a big navy. Four years after his move, the whole of eastern Sicily was threatened by invasion from Carthage. Gelon overwhelmingly defeated the Carthaginians at precisely the time when his fellow-Greeks in the Aegean destroyed the Persian fleet at Salamis. This gave Syracuse something of the stature in the eyes of the Greeks of Sicily that Athens and Sparta together had in the eyes of the Greeks of the Aegean.

Gelon was the eldest of four brothers, sons of a certain Deinomenes, and when he died he was succeeded as ruler of Syracuse by the second of the four, Hieron. They were what the Greeks called 'tyrants', a word which for us connotes the cruel and oppressive exercise of power; a Greek 'tyrant' could indeed be cruel and oppressive (hence 'tyranny' was a bogy-word to democracies and aristocracies alike), but he was not necessarily so. There were tyrannies which championed and protected the poor against the rich, tyrannies which patronised the arts, instituted festivals, and built splendid buildings. The Sicilian tyrants revealed their pride in being Greeks and their ambition to be admired and honoured throughout the Greek world by dedicating spoils of victory in the sanctuary of Zeus at Olympia and the sanctuary of Apollo at Delphi. They entered teams for the chariot-races in the games at Olympia and Delphi, and usually won; the famous bronze charioteer in the Delphi museum is the surviving piece of a great bronze group, chariot and horses and all, dedicated by the third of the Deinomenid brothers, Polyzalos. Hieron invited to his court the greatest poets of his day, and they came gladly: Simonides, Pindar, Aeschylus. Pindar composed songs in celebration of Hieron's victories at the games, and Aeschylus wrote a set of plays for performance at Syracuse commemorating the foundation of the new city of Aitna. Surprising, at first sight; we might have expected Pindar, born and bred in the governing class of Thebes, and Aeschylus, citizen of an increasingly radical democracy, to have hesitated on ideological grounds from accepting the patronage of a tyrant. But although Aeschylus or Pindar would have resisted by force any attempt to establish a tyranny in his own city, they both recognised that an opportunity to seize power was a temptation to which any man might yield; and once power is taken, prudence forbids that it be relinquished. Also, like most Greeks, they looked more to the good that a man accomplished than to the morality of his intentions.

To become an enemy of a Greek ruler was hardly less dangerous than to become an enemy of an Egyptian or Assyrian king, but there was an extraordinary difference of style and tone in the Greek ruler's exercise of power. Listen to the bloodthirsty exultation, the confidence in divine patronage, which resound in the royal inscriptions of Egypt and Assyria.

> With the supreme might of the god Nergal who marches before me, with the terrible weapons which Aššur my lord supplied, I fought with them and defeated them. Their warriors I overthrew with the sword, like the god Ramman I rained a deluge upon them, into trenches I heaped them, with the corpses of their mighty men I filled the broad plain, with their blood I dyed the mountain like scarlet wool....
>
> A pile of heads against his city I set, his cities I overthrew, I destroyed, I burnt with fire.
>
> At that time I celebrated the might of the great gods and I made glorious for all time the power of Aššur and Šamaš. My royal image of great size I made; my heroic acts and my victorious deeds I inscribed thereon; and at the source of the river Saluara at the foot of the mountains of Amanus I set it up.
>
> (Shalmaneser II of Assyria)[20]

> His majesty has gone forth like a whirlwind against them, fighting on the battlefield like a runner. The dread of him and the terror of him have entered into their bodies. They are capsized and overwhelmed where they are. Their heart is taken away, their soul is flown away. Their weapons are scattered upon the sea. His arrow pierces whom of them he may have wished, and the fugitive is become one fallen into the water. His majesty is like an enraged lion, attacking his assailants with his arms: plundering on his right hand and powerful on his left hand, like Seth destroying the serpent 'Evil of Character'.
>
> (Ramses III of Egypt)[21]

Greeks liked winning fights, too, and they liked to be praised for winning, but they distrusted gross flattery and shrank from exaggerated boasting. When they won, they were inclined to think that gods had favoured them and deserved thanks, but they knew that gods were arbitrary and unpredictable. They knew too that even the richest and most powerful of rulers may come to a miserable end. When Hieron won a great naval battle over the Etruscans off Kyme, he dedicated a helmet as a thank-offering to Zeus at Olympia. It can be seen in the British Museum, and the inscription on it says simply:

> Hieron, son of Deinomenes, and the Syracusans
> to Zeus
> Etruscan (*sc.* spoils)
> from Kyme.[22]

The helmet dedicated at Olympia by Hieron of Syracuse after his victory over the Etruscans and Carthaginians off Kyme. The dialect, spelling and script are, naturally enough, Syracusan.

### Democracy

The Deinomenid family, for all their magnificence, had only a short run, twenty years, for soon after Hieron's death his successor, Thrasyboulos, the youngest of the quartet of brothers, was overthrown, and for two generations Syracuse became, like Athens, a democracy.

'Democracy' is the Greek *dēmokratiā*, 'exercise of power by the whole people', but what a Greek meant by 'the whole people' is not quite what we mean. He meant the adult male citizens, and citizenship was a set of rights which a man inherited from his father; gifts of citizenship to individuals were unusual, and the incorporation of whole groups of people at a time was an exceptional measure. Democracy was government by a mass assembly which excluded women, children, foreigners (whether residents or temporary visitors) and, of course, slaves; so it was very far from being government of a place by all the human beings who lived and worked there.

Greek democracy has had a bad press, on the whole, because the most famous and influential writers of political theory, Plato and Aristotle, were hostile to it. Thucydides, too, historian of the Athenian and Syracusan democracies at war, is at best critical and on occasion hostile. We have to construct democratic political theory out of the implications of historical events and out of political speeches which show democracy at work; there is no democratic theorist to help us. There is, however, one famous passage, constantly retranslated and quoted, from which we can see directly what a champion of democracy might say about it. This comes from the 'Funeral Speech' which Thucydides, in his history, puts into the mouth of Perikles on the occasion of the public funeral of the Athenians killed during the first year of the Peloponnesian War. We don't know how much it resembles what Perikles actually said on that occasion, because Thucydides casts all the speeches of all his characters into the same extraordinarily condensed and sophisticated language, full of abstract reasoning. In the translation I have simplified the structure of the original sentences and have spelled out some implications in order to make the argument clear.

> Our system of government does not emulate our neighbour's institutions. So far from imitating others, we are ourselves a model. Our system is called 'democracy' because the city is controlled not by a small class but by the majority.
>
> The law gives everyone equal rights, recognised in settling disputes between individuals.
>
> Some men are respected more; and whenever a man is known to be good at something, it does not matter what section of the population he comes from; he gains advancement in public life according to his quality.
>
> Some men are poor; but if a man can do the city some good, he is not prevented from doing it by the lowliness of his status.
>
> We act as free men both in the conduct of public business and in the way we look at one another's everyday behaviour. We do not get angry with our neighbour if he sometimes does what he enjoys, nor do we show resentment which looks disagreeable even when it inflicts no damage.
>
> Dealing with one another in a way which avoids offence, we refrain from violation of the law in our capacity as citizens – through fear, above all, obeying whoever is at any given time in office, and obeying the laws, particularly those which have been made for the protection of the victim and those unwritten laws which are respected by common assent.[23]

These are not the words of a social historian making a cool assessment of Athenian democracy. They are a proud boast, spoken by an orator on a ceremonial occasion. Like the majority of boasts, they are at least in part untrue; it is easy to point to occurrences, or even to constant elements, in the history of the Athenian democracy which are incompatible with Perikles' generalisations about it. But if we know what people like to be told about themselves, we have learned something of great importance about them; how far they measure up to their own ideals is a separate question.

The ideals of Athenian democracy are not to be dismissed as a sham solely on the grounds that women were excluded from the making of political decisions, or on the grounds that the economy of Athens rested on an immense amount of slave labour. The Greeks were not acquainted with any society which admitted men and women on equal terms to deliberations affecting the community, or with any society which did not use slaves. Eventually a few Greeks from time to time called in question the way in which the total human population of a city-state was exploited by its adult male citizens. Even if there were no such voices to be heard, it would still be unreasonable to criticise Greek civilisation as a whole as if it had invented or intensified that exploitation. If we are to throw the Greeks out of the window because they had slaves, shall we not throw most of the human race out with them? If we condemn slavery, what are we to say of caste in India? At least slaves could be freed, and often were, but no act of generosity could move a family from a lower to a higher caste. And what are we to say of conditions which are very different from slavery in the eyes of the jurist or the economic historian, but not all that different as an experience at the receiving end? I think, for example, of my great-grandfather, orphaned in 1848 and going to work in a factory at the age of eleven, where he was lashed across the back by the foreman if he grew dozy at the end of a long day.

Whoever regards the exploitation of the weaker by the stronger as the greatest of evils will see a grey fog of evil stretching over practically all the history of our species. Here and there is a glow, sometimes even a gleam, of a new idea which may in time disperse some of the fog. These are the exciting things in the study of history. There is a constellation of gleams in Greek history, and the development of democratic government is among them. In common with scientific speculation and artistic experiment, it was a product of a characteristically Greek refusal to take traditional practice for granted. First one stratum of a citizen-population, then another, dug its heels in and insisted on a share in the machinery of political decision. There was no absolutely clear-cut dividing line between democracy and its antithesis, 'oligarchy'. If only the richest ten per cent of the citizens had power, that was obviously oligarchy, and if all had equal power, that was obviously democracy; but many intermediate stages existed in different parts of the Greek world, stages which one might call 'broad-based oligarchy' or 'limited democracy'. The situation is complicated by the existence in some cities of categories other than 'citizen' and 'non-citizen'. The exercise of political decision might rest with a small class calling themselves 'citizens', uncompromisingly egalitarian in their dealings with one another; but if they excluded from power large classes who were neither foreigners nor slaves, one would hesitate to call their system a democracy.

Citizens were seldom directly employed by other citizens in return for wages, since owners of land or workshops or lessees of mines used slave-labour, whether or not they also worked with their own hands. Consequently conflict between capital and labour, in the modern sense, was absent from an ancient democracy. Conflict between rich and poor was by no means absent, but it turned upon the claims made on the wealth of the minority by the state as employer, patron, and benefactor of the majority. Ancient democracies were not angelic. A crowd can be as intolerant and oppressive as a tyrant, and equally impatient of considerations of justice when it sees its own interests threatened.

To build great temples, stage beautiful festivals, or ensure the working of the democratic system by offering pay for public service, a city-state needed more money than it was willing to raise by taxing its own inhabitants. One way of acquiring money was to take it from others by the threat of force. That was the financial basis of the Athenian Empire and the achievements of Athens during her imperial period: annual payment of tribute by the subject-allies of Athens. To say that the exaction of tribute called for the maintenance of a big navy and the maintenance of a big navy called for the exaction of tribute is a brutal and cynical truth, but only part of the truth. The Athenian navy was created in response to the growing threat from Persia, not in order to subjugate other Greeks; the ships were paid for initially by a rich vein in the silver-mines on Attic soil, not by tribute; they were the decisive factor in the defeat of the Persian invasion; and in the immediate aftermath of the war the navy was maintained with the enthusiastic co-operation of Athens' allies, to ensure that the Persians were kept as far away from the Greek world as possible. As the Persian threat faded to vanishing-point, a new threat came into focus: the polarisation of Greece around Athens and around Sparta. Self-protection became the justification for the big navy and the exaction of tribute, the tightening control over 'allies' which turned them into subjects, and the ruthless suppression of attempts to secede. Near the end of his life, Perikles told the Athenian people: 'Your empire is by now like a tyranny. Men think it wrong to take such power – but dangerous to let it go.'[24]

In a passage of the Funeral Speech which comes some time after the passage quoted above, Perikles says: 'We shall be admired by future generations as we are admired now.' Well, true, that has turned out to be so; but admired for what? Tolerance, compassion, respect for law? Not, at any rate, in this passage, for he continues:

> They have plenty to go on: we have ensured that there is no lack of witnesses to our power. We need no Homer to praise us, no poet to make an impression of heroic deeds in verses which give the audience pleasure for a moment but do not really stand up to scrutiny. We have laid every sea and every land open to our daring; everywhere we have created eternal monuments of triumph and suffering.[25]

He is speaking here of the restless, aggressive courage which took Athenian warships and troops not only to fight the Persians in Cyprus and Egypt but also to crush rebellious allies and consolidate Athenian wealth and power. Nothing of importance is achieved without unselfishness, of which courage, tenacity, and endurance of suffering are species, and there is no reason to withhold admiration from these virtues merely because we disapprove of the cause in which they are displayed. No one should pause to remember his own nationality before he can respond adequately to the story of Arnhem, of Cassino, or of Stalingrad. Proud of the qualities which enabled them to acquire an empire, the Athenians did not question the morality of acquisition.

When the Peloponnesian War had begun, the Athenians suffered two great blows, one sudden and dramatic, the other slow and grim. The sudden blow was the great plague which killed one third of the population. The other was the inescapable fact that the war devoured their reserves of accumulated tribute at a frightening rate. Just at the time when this had become past ignoring or explaining away, the city of Mytilene on the island of Lesbos, the most important of their subject-allies, rebelled. The rebellion was suppressed, and the Athenian assembly took the decision to kill the entire adult male citizen population of Mytilene. So cruel a decision aroused strong emotions, and the issue was reopened in a second debate. Thucydides presents this debate to us as a pair of highly-wrought speeches, one by Kleon, the most influential man in Athenian politics at the time, and the other by Diodotos, of whom we otherwise hear nothing. Kleon urges adherence to the original decision. He reproaches his audience by observing, in his opening words, that 'a democracy is incapable of ruling over other states', because the citizens of a democracy, accustomed to being nice to one another, ready to change their decisions, and captivated by clever argument in debate, do not take seriously enough the tenacious malice of external enemies. Compassion and good-heartedness are disastrous, he says, in an imperial power. If you are soft, you will be despised, and your enemies will take heart. He sums up:

> If you do as I say, you'll be acting rightly towards Mytilene, and at the same time acting in your own interests. If you decide otherwise, you still won't turn the Mytileneans into friends, and you'll be passing an adverse verdict on yourselves. If they were right to revolt, it follows that your rule is wrong. If you decide to go on ruling, even when you ought not to, Mytilene has got to be punished in the way your interest requires – and never mind about equity; otherwise, you should give up your empire, run away from risks, be virtuous.[26]

Diodotos in his reply is very careful not to expose himself to the sneer with which that passage from Kleon's speech ends, for he insists:

*Don't* be swayed by pity or good-heartedness. I'm *not* saying that those should be your motives.

So:

> If I prove the Mytileneans guilty of enormous injury, that doesn't mean that I must urge you to kill them, if it's not in our interest to do so. If I prove that they deserve forgiveness, I don't for that reason say, 'Forgive them', if it's not a good thing for Athens.[27]

If we kill the Mytileneans, he argues, it won't deter other subject-allies from revolting, because people are not always rational; they revolt in the conviction that they are going to succeed. And if, once they have revolted, they know there's no hope of coming to terms, they'll fight to the death. And then, when we've won and killed them all, we're left with an empty city which can never pay tribute again.

The vote went in favour of Diodotos; the Mytileneans were reprieved. Modern readers are shocked by the terms in which the debate is conducted, and tend either to blame Thucydides for what they assume to be his own determination to misrepresent historical issues by ignoring the heart and considering only the head, or to blame the Athenian people as a whole, on the assumption that Diodotos won for the reasons which Thucydides puts into his mouth, and for no other reasons. Quite apart from the fact that our hearts are often crueller than our heads, especially when we taste the joy of revenge, neither assumption is justified. Diodotos has a particular argument to answer, and he answers it by meeting Kleon on Kleon's own ground. He does not need to use the argument from sentiment, for, as readers of Thucydides sometimes fail to notice, it was the existence of sentiment which had caused the debate to be reopened in the first place:

> Next day they had a sudden change of heart, considering on reflection that their decision had been an extraordinarily cruel one – to destroy a whole city rather than simply the guilty. So another assembly was immediately convened.[28]

Athens survived the crises of the first ten years of her great war with Sparta. An uneasy peace was made. In the course of those first ten years, Athens had turned her eyes westwards, persuading herself that it might be possible to bring the Greek states of Sicily within the empire. She tried, by intervening with an expeditionary force in their local wars, to build up a system of alliances against Syracuse. That attempt failed; in fact, it had the effect of pushing the Sicilian Greeks into a fragile but momentarily impressive unity. But in 415 Athens was tempted to intervene again; the prospect of turning all those rich cities into tribute-paying allies, giving herself a much bigger financial reserve in readiness for the inevitable resumption of war with Sparta, was enticing. A certain contempt for the

Greeks of Sicily played its part in reinforcing the Athenians' ambition.

So the biggest, wealthiest democracy of the Aegean moved into conflict with the biggest, wealthiest democracy of the West. Both had a proud tradition of leadership against 'barbarian' invaders. Both derived their wealth in part from indirect taxation of commerce, in part from tribute – Athens from her subject-allies, Syracuse from the native peoples of her hinterland. But for once Athens could not rely on a weapon which at other times and places had served her well, the sympathy of the ordinary people in the states which she attacked, for Syracuse was already a democratic city and had no occasion to think of Athenian victory as a political liberation.

### The Sicilian Disaster

We call it the 'Sicilian Disaster', which befell the 'Sicilian Expedition'. Looked at from the other end, we could call it the 'Syracusan Triumph', which ended the 'Athenian Invasion'.

The Athenian expedition which was intended to subjugate Sicily left Athens in the summer of 415 BC. It was an impressive force, by Greek standards, in size, equipment, and training: sixty Athenian warships and eighty other ships (Athenian and allied together) carrying over five thousand heavy infantry and thirteen hundred light troops. In accordance with Athenian democratic practice, the force was commanded by three elected generals, of equal authority. Divided command seldom works well, and on this occasion the division was not merely formal. One of the three generals, Nikias, thought the expedition a bad strategic error, and had argued against it vigorously when it was first discussed in the Athenian assembly. A second general, Alkibiades, sailed with serious charges of blasphemy hanging over him, and he suspected (rightly) that in his absence his numerous enemies would build up a prejudice against him which would not simply end his career but endanger his life.

On arrival at the toe of Italy the third general, Lamakhos, argued for a direct and speedy attack on Syracuse itself. Nikias' reluctance to take risks amounted to sabotage of the essential purpose of the expedition. Alkibiades preferred to delay the attack on Syracuse until they had secured support from as many as possible of the other Greek cities in Sicily. When each of three generals puts forward a different plan, nothing can happen until one of them backs down and gives his vote for one of the others. That is how Nikias, Alkibiades, and Lamakhos resolved the issue; Lamakhos, who was inferior to the other two in political standing, yielded to Alkibiades' view, and the three generals proceeded to carry out a plan in which only one of them had any faith. Halfway through, Alkibiades was recalled to Athens to stand trial, and on the way home he prudently disappeared. Now an enemy of his motherland, he went to

One of the surviving fragments of a set of Athenian decrees which made detailed provision for the expedition to Sicily in 415 BC. The strict chequer-board pattern, without punctuation or gaps between words, was generally favoured in Athenian documents on aesthetic grounds. In 403 BC their official spelling was changed to something more familiar to modern learners of Greek.

Sparta to urge the Spartans to act against Athens in support of Syracuse.

For one reason and another, things went wrong with the Athenian force in Sicily. They failed to get much of the good will and practical help they had hoped for. Before the winter set in, they defeated the Syracusans in a pitched battle close by the city, but could not follow up their victory, because the Syracusans were strong in cavalry and they were not. So they withdrew for the winter to a friendly city on the east coast of Sicily, and only in the spring re-established themselves at Syracuse and began to build siege-walls to cut off completely the city's landward communications. The best part of the summer went by, and they were within a very narrow distance of putting Syracuse into a hopeless predicament, when the situation was transformed by the arrival of an experienced Spartan commander, Gylippos, who evaded the Athenian naval patrol which had hoped to stop him. Gylippos' arrival instantly raised Syracusan morale, and his military skill thwarted the Athenians' completion of their siege operations. In answer to a gloomy despatch from Nikias (Lamakhos had meanwhile been killed in battle) the Athenians, so far from deciding to withdraw, prepared reinforcements on a grand scale, which eventually arrived at Syracuse in the summer of 413 BC.

33

The moral effect of their arrival was, for a moment, considerable, but not decisive. By that time the Syracusans had had the best of it in most of the fighting on land, and, what was far more important, they had dared to pit their ships against the Athenian ships in the great harbour – successfully, thanks to intelligent adaptation of their tactics to a sea-battle in a confined space. A trireme was rather like the fuselage of a Boeing 707, powered in battle by 180 rowers and fitted at the prow with an iron-clad ram. The object of manœuvre was to ram the enemy trireme in the stern or amidships. The Syracusans strengthened their prows massively and sought head-on or glancing impact. Thus they proved to themselves, and to the rest of the Greek world, that the Athenian fleet was not invincible. Now the Athenians attempted, with the massive reinforcements at their disposal, to capture the whole of the plateau above the city in a surprise attack by night. The attack failed disastrously, and from then on the initiative lay wholly with the Syracusans. The issue was no longer whether the Athenians could take Syracuse but whether the Syracusans could prevent the Athenians from ever returning to Greece. Perhaps they could not have done, if the Athenians had withdrawn without a moment's delay, but a singular delay was in fact imposed. There was an eclipse of the moon – it was 27 August, 413, a little more than two years after the Athenians' arrival in Sicily – and the Athenian rank and file took this to be a divine veto on their intended withdrawal. The professional seers demanded a delay of 'thrice nine days'.

The Syracusans, who did not interpret the eclipse as any impediment to *their* plans, now blocked the exit from the harbour by ships anchored broadside-on. It was hopeless for the Athenians to pack their entire force on to their remaining ships and get clear away before the Syracusan warships were upon them. They must – somehow – win a decisive naval victory within the harbour, which would enable them to unblock the harbour-mouth and keep it open, and *then* evacuate their forces. Thucydides describes this critical battle:

> When the Athenians came up against the barrier, with the impetus of that first onslaught they overpowered the ships stationed in front of the barrier and tried to break through what held them in. Thereupon the Syracusans and their allies bore down on them from every quarter; and now the fighting was no longer only at the barrier, but in every part of the harbour.[29]

I suppose that by now I must have read this part of Thucydides' text more than a hundred times; I have published a commentary on books vi and vii, which involved me in some six thousand hours of work altogether, much of it on the minutiae of chronology, grammar, and textual criticism (for example, I once looked up all six hundred examples of a certain common preposition in the whole of Thucydides in order to elucidate the precise sense of one passage). Yet I still cannot read the words 'thereupon the Syracusans and their allies bore down on them from every quarter' without feeling the hair on the back on my neck stand on end, as when in a war-film a great attacking force suddenly begins to move, full of vengeful confidence. Perhaps that is why I don't mind interrupting Thucydides to talk about prepositions and the like. He is still there when I come back to him.

> It was a violent battle, more than any of those that had preceded it. The rowers on both sides made every effort to attack whenever they were told to, and the officers used all their skill against their adversaries and in rivalry with one another. Whenever one ship came up against another the marines on board took care that what they did from the deck should measure up to the skill of the sailors; every single man, whatever the job allotted to him, was anxious to be seen to excel at it. Many ships were crowded in conflict in a small space; never had so many ships fought a battle in such confinement, for the number of both sides added together was not far short of two hundred. There were not many ramming attacks, since there was no room to back or to sail through and turn about; collisions were much more frequent, one ship crashing into another accidentally in trying to extricate itself or to attack someone else. While one ship was bearing down on another, the men on the decks made lavish use of javelins, arrows and stones; and when contact was made, the marines tried to board the enemy and fight hand-to-hand.

'In *rivalry* with one another', 'anxious to be *seen to excel*': a reputation for valour was the surest immortality, and a Greek community believed that its own interests were best served by prizes and awards. A Greek who got a public commendation did not mumble modestly, 'I only did my duty'. He knew that everyone knew that he strove for pre-eminence and recognition.

After another page on the fighting between ships, Thucydides continues:

> While the issue of the battle on the water was still in the balance, there was great anguish and conflict in the hearts of the armies of both sides on land – the Syracusans ambitious to win greater glory even than before, and the invaders afraid of finding themselves worse off than they already were....
>
> As the struggle went on indecisively, the Athenian soldiers revealed the fear in their hearts by the swaying of their bodies; it was a time of agony for them, for escape or destruction seemed every moment just at hand. So long as the issue of the sea-battle was in doubt, you could have heard every kind of sound in one place, the Athenian camp: lamentation, shouting, 'We're winning!', 'We're losing!', all the cries wrung from a great army in great peril. The feelings of the men on the ships was much the same, until at last, when the battle had gone on for

a long time, the Syracusans and their allies routed the Athenians and fell upon them, decisive winners, yelling and cheering, and chased them to the land. And then the Athenian sailors, as many of them as had not been captured afloat, beached their ships wherever they could and poured into the camp. The soldiers were not in two minds any more, but all with one impulse, groaning, wailing, lamenting the outcome of the battle, rallied – some of them close to the ships, others to guard the rest of their defensive wall, while the greater part of them began to think now about themselves, about how they were going to survive.

The Athenians were doomed to an attempt to get away by land, hungry and thirsty, exhausted, dispirited. They left behind their sick and wounded, who crawled or hobbled in their wake for a little while. Harassed by the enemy, their way blocked wherever the Syracusans could block it for a time without too costly a battle, they struck inland, then doubled back to the coast and went southwards. They were looking for friends, but unlikely to find any now that they were beaten and desperate; and they had rivers to cross, one after another. Their force was divided in two; a gap opened between the two halves, and the rear half, surrounded, gave up. The half that Nikias led reached the Assinaros, a small river in a steep-sided gully, and this was the end.

The Athenians hurried on towards the river Assinaros, under pressure from attacks made on all sides by the very numerous Syracusan cavalry and crowds of skirmishers. They felt that they would find things easier if they could get across the river; and at the same time their sufferings and lust for water drove them on. When they reached the river, they rushed into it, and now all discipline was gone. Every man wanted to be the first across, and the enemy's attacks made the crossing difficult. Forced into a tight mass, they collided and trampled one another down; some were killed at once by spears and equipment, others got entangled and carried away by the river. The Syracusans, lined up on the other side of the river, where the bank was steep, hurled missiles from above on to the Athenians, most of whom were drinking greedily and in total disorder at the bottom of the gully. And the Peloponnesian allies of Syracuse came down and concentrated on killing those who were in the river. The water was fouled at once, but they drank it none the less, a mess of mud and blood; indeed, most of them fought over it.[30]

So Nikias and the survivors surrendered. The Syracusans herded the prisoners back to Syracuse and penned them in the deep quarries adjoining the city.

The men in the quarries were treated badly by the Syracusans during the first period of their captivity. The place was deep and narrow, and many were crowded into it. At first the sunshine and continuing heat oppressed them, for there was no roof; and then the cold autumn nights came on, a change which generated sickness. Since they did everything in the same place, for lack of room, and also the corpses of those who died from wounds or through the change of climate or some such cause were all heaped one on top of another, the stench was unbearable; and they were tormented moreover by hunger and thirst, for the Syracusans gave each man, for eight months, half a pint of water and a pint of grain a day. Of all the sufferings that it could be expected men cast into such a place would undergo, there was not one that did not afflict them.[31]

Thucydides brings his long narrative of the Athenian expedition to an end in a resounding climax:

This was in fact the greatest military achievement in the Peloponnesian War and, in my view, the greatest in Greek history – for the victors the most decisive, for the vanquished the most catastrophic; for they were defeated totally, in every way; nothing that they suffered was on an ordinary scale; army, fleet, everything was destroyed, as they say, root and branch, and few out of many came home to Athens.[32]

In real life – by contrast with a story which the writer can stop when he pleases – climax is apt to be followed by anticlimax. The Greek world had been taken aback by the scale and splendour of the expedition that left Athens in 415. It was thunderstruck when a year and a half later the Athenians sent out reinforcements comparable in scale with the original expedition. And when in the autumn of 413 'everything was destroyed, root and branch, and few out of many came home to Athens', everyone thought that Athens was finished. Her subject-allies would rebel, she would not have the power to suppress rebellion, no tribute would come in, and the handful of ships she could scrape up would not prevent the Peloponnesians from severing her lifeline, the commercial route that brought her food from the Black Sea. Not for the first time, Athens was saved by her own resolute energy and by complacency, delay and dissension among her enemies. Some of her allies rebelled, certainly, but the Athenians responded so vigorously that within two years of the disaster in Sicily it was plain that Athens was *not* finished; she *could* still win the war against the Peloponnesians. Indeed, she nearly did. It was not until 405 that one great sea-battle in the Hellespont, which links the Mediterranean to the Black Sea, settled the issue. Athens *could* have won that battle, but lost it. Had she won it, as she had won a battle on a comparable scale the year before, the chances are that the Peloponnesians would have been willing to concede a great deal for the sake of peace.

So, for all that it seemed to Thucydides 'the greatest military achievement in Greek history', the Triumph of Syracuse is not to be classed among the 'decisive' battles of the world. It is more important in Greek literature than it is in Greek history, for Thucydides chose to devote to it more space than to any other period of comparable length in the

Peloponnesian War, and to lavish on it all the narrative and rhetorical skill of which he was capable. Among the many things that make his account of it worth reading and re-reading we might pick on his revelation of what Greek warfare was like as an experience. I would not attach so much importance to that, though; blood and shit and pus are the same, and pain and fear similar, in all ages, and I have gained a great deal in understanding Thucydides from having been a participant in a demoralised retreat 2354 years after the Athenian retreat from Syracuse. I am more interested in *how* he describes war than in *what* he describes. We have already seen how Aeschylus, putting a vivid account of the battle of Salamis into the mouth of a Persian, detaches himself from his natural standpoint as a Greek and looks at the event through the eyes of his enemies. At the same time – and this is in particularly striking contrast to Oriental war-narratives – he thinks and speaks in collective terms, of Greeks and Asiatics, not of named kings and generals and admirals. Thucydides treats his story of the last battle in the harbour at Syracuse in the same way. It is pointless to ask, 'Which side is he on?', because he did his best throughout his history to make that question hard to answer. It is equally pointless to ask, '*Whose* victory was it?', expecting individuals to be named, because once he has named the commanders of the main sections of the two fleets (in the paragraph preceding 'When the Athenians came up against the barrier . . .') he allows them to drop out of sight and out of mind. Everything that follows is expressed in terms of collective action and collective suffering. That is a general feature of Greek narrative, whether the battle in question is real or mythical. A few years before the Athenian expedition to Sicily Euripides put on his tragedy *Suppliants* (or *Suppliant Women*), in the course of which an Athenian messenger described a mythical victory of Athens over Thebes. It is a very long speech (ninety lines), and strongly Homeric in character: the tide is turned in favour of Athens by her king Theseus, who strikes off enemy heads right and left with his club, and, as befits a battle in the 'heroic age', chariots play a spectacular part in the battle, though Euripides and Homer alike failed to understand how chariots had really been used in battle. At one point the Messenger says:

> This is no hearsay,
> I saw it all myself, for I was there –
> the turmoil of the chariots and the soldiers,
> a sea of pain! What can I tell first?
> The swirl of dust that rose to touch the sky?
> Or men entangled in their reins and tossed
> this way and that, and bloody trails of red –
> some falling, others hurled in somersaults,
> their chariots smashed, their heads cracked on the ground,
> all lifeless in the wreckage?[33]

The ingredients of the description are in part conventional ('I saw it all myself' and 'What can I tell first?'), in part dictated by reality (a battle in dry weather does raise a swirl of dust to 'touch the sky'), but it is noteworthy that in such a context it did not matter to the poet and his audience *whose* 'pain' is being described, or *which* charioteers were hurled from their vehicles. Greatly though he exults in the victory of Athens at the end of his speech, the Athenian messenger can stand back and look at the embroilment of his own side with the enemy as a scene full of drama and pathos in its own right.

### A Question in a Quarry

A visitor to the Syracusan quarries, not beset, as the Athenian prisoners were, by sickness, pain and starvation, has leisure to notice that the limestone is full of fossils. In the days before the timescale of the history of living beings on earth was understood, there were three ways in which people could react to the sight of (for example) a fossil fish. They could say, 'Isn't it funny, that bit of rock looks just like a fish!', and get back to thinking about what they would have for supper. Or, 'A miracle! God has put a fish in the rock!' Or they could say, 'Well, now, I wonder . . .'. A certain Xenophanes, some time in the late 500s BC, said to himself, 'I wonder . . .', and drew the conclusion that the distribution of land and water had not always been what it was in his time; every so often, he suggested, they had combined to form a world of mud, then separated out again, and fossils were the imprints retained by mud which had become solid.[34]

Xenophanes came from Kolophon, on the coast of Asia Minor, but he migrated to Sicily and South Italy when his native region came under Persian rule, and he may have spent most of his life there. He turned his mind to a great variety of topics, and, in accordance with the normal practice of his time, cast his opinions on all those topics into poetry. We possess it only in tantalisingly short passages quoted by later authors, or through brief allusions which may or may not do justice to what he actually said. The quoted passages – one of which comes from a poem composed, he says, when he was ninety-two years old – suggest that he was by no means a naturally gifted poet, but the ideas they communicate are exciting. Down to his time, the men whose activity we could bring under the heading of 'philosophy', if we were pretty generous in the interpretation of that word, devoted themselves either to exhortation and moralising within a generally accepted framework of values, or to quasi-scientific speculation about how the universe began. A hundred years after his time, philosophers concerned themselves much more with what Socrates called 'no ordinary question: *how should one live?*', and they tackled this question by much more penetrating criticism of accepted social and political values. Xenophanes continued the old tradition of speculation about the universe, but he also anticipated the moral preoccupations of Socrates and Plato. What binds these two lines of thought together is enquiry into the nature of God, and on that subject Xenophanes had some remarkable observations to make.

> The Ethiopians say that their gods are snub-nosed and black; and the Thracians, that theirs are blue-eyed and red-haired.[35]

The implication is not 'What a pity that the Ethiopians and Thracians don't know any better!', but 'So how can we Greeks be so sure we know what gods look like?' Or, indeed, 'How can *humans* be so sure?'

> If oxen and horses and lions had hands with which to paint and make the works of art that men make, horses would paint gods resembling horses, and oxen gods resembling oxen, making the bodies of the gods just like the bodies of their own species.[36]

As for the myths which reflected most people's idea of gods in action:

> Homer and Hesiod attributed to the gods everything which among men is blamed and reproached – theft and adultery and deceit.[37]

Xenophanes simply threw myth overboard, rejecting as 'fictions of our forebears' all stories of conflict and war between supernatural powers. In place of the gods whom man has made both physically and morally in his own image, Xenophanes posited:

> One god ..., not like mortal beings either in body or in mind,

of whom he said:

> The whole of him sees; the whole of him thinks; the whole of him hears.[38]

A doctrine which undermines the foundations of poetry, art, festivals and folklore might be expected to create quite a disturbance in the society in which it is preached. And Xenophanes deliberately hit another sensitive nerve in suggesting that the Greek cities were mistaken to make such a fuss of athletes. Strength, toughness and speed, he said, don't contribute as much as 'my understanding' to making a city prosperous and secure. The word he used, *sophia*, is not quite 'wisdom', but rather the understanding of something which calls for natural intelligence and sensitivity, skill and practice. The great artist has it; so does the great poet or scientist or administrator.

No one, so far as we know, ever tried to prosecute Xenophanes for blasphemy or to frame him on some other charge which would silence his disquieting social criticism. And clearly, if anyone ever tried to ban or burn his writings, the attempt was unsuccessful, for they were obtainable for centuries after his death and were treated with neither more nor less respect than the writings of his contemporaries. 'Orthodoxy' and 'dogma' happen to be Greek words in origin, but the things they denote were quite alien to the outlook of Greeks in the pre-Christian period. There was no religious authority sufficiently well organised and influential to demand and enforce universal acceptance of a set of beliefs. Save in some sects and cults outside the mainstream of Greek history, there were no texts treated as sacred and inspired. The old saying, 'Homer was the Bible of the Greeks', is a half-truth, or a quarter-truth, in so far as the *Iliad* and the *Odyssey* were more widely known than other texts and more often quoted in conversation to make a point, but no one treated them as 'the Word of God'. There was a general tendency to believe that great poets owed their skill and their apparent knowledge of the remote past to the inspiration of supernatural beings, the Muses, and naturally the poets themselves exploited this conventional belief. But different poets in different localities told irreconcilable versions of the same myth, from which it followed necessarily that, although one or other of a set of versions *might* be true, all but one *must* be false and conceivably *all* were false. There was no established canon accepted for many generations and then suddenly questioned in an age of sophistication and scepticism. The existence of irreconcilable myths was a fact of life from the very beginning; mythology was a creative activity, each individual poet selecting, modifying and inventing. When Hesiod tells the story of his own meeting with the Muses in a lonely place, a meeting at which they endowed him with poetic skill, he makes them say:

> We know how to tell fiction which resembles truth; and we know how to declare truth, when we wish.[39]

Given the absence of any religious authority which could impose on hundreds of independent city-states one creation-story, one belief about the after-life, or one set of theological propositions, the way was open for the individual not only to speculate (for individuals have always been able to do that) but also to express the opinions to which his speculation led him. When the earliest Greeks confronted the question, 'How did the world begin?', they answered it in terms of supernatural persons, modelling the relations between the elements of nature on human family histories. So, for example, Hesiod in his *Theogony*:

> The Gulf of Space came into being first of all, and thereafter Earth, broad of bosom, abode for ever sure for all the immortal gods who possess the peak of snowy Olympos; and misty Tartaros, in a recess below the wide ways of the land; and Love, most beautiful of all the immortal gods, Love who makes us tremble in our limbs; he overpowers the mind and wise counsel in the breasts of all gods and all mankind. From Space came Erebos and black Night, and from Night in turn Day and Air came forth, whom she conceived from making love with Erebos. And Earth gave birth first of all to starry Sky, equal to herself, that he might cover her all over, and to be an abode for ever sure for

the blessed gods. Then she brought forth long Mountains, the lovely dwellings of goddesses, the Nymphs, who live in mountain glens. Then without the delight of love she bore the barren waters, raging, swollen, the great Sea. And then she lay with Sky, and bore Ocean, deep-swirling, and Koios, then Kreios, Iapetos, Hyperion, Thea, Rhea, Themis, Mnemosyne, Phoebe, golden-crowned, and lovely Tethys. After them, Kronos was born, wily in wits, most formidable of her children; and he was the enemy of his vigorous father. Then again she bore the Cyclopses arrogant in spirit, Brontes and Steropes and fierce-hearted Arges, those who gave thunder to Zeus and forged his lightning. They were like the gods in all else, but each had a single eye set in mid-forehead; and the name 'Cyclopses' was given to them because one circular eye was set in their forehead. And in their works were strength and power and skill.[40]

Come down now to the time of Xenophanes, getting on for two hundred years after Hesiod, and we hear a very different note in what we are told about a certain Anaximandros:

Anaximandros said that the first living creatures were generated in water, encased in spiny coverings. As they matured, they emerged on to drier ground....

And, according to another of our limited sources of information on Anaximandros' theories:

Inside these fish-like creatures human beings formed and were retained as foetuses until the age of puberty. Then the coverings burst and men and women came forth, capable of feeding themselves.[41]

From asking, 'How did things *begin*?', it is a single step to asking, 'How do things work *now*?', and a hundred years after Anaximandros we find a notable intellectual of the Classical period, Anaxagoras, saying:

Everyone has the wrong conception of 'coming into being' and 'perishing', for nothing comes into being, nor does it perish, but it is put together from things already existing and taken apart again. So they ought to speak of 'being taken apart' instead of 'perishing'.[42]

Hesiod's roll-call of divine and monstrous beings, loving and hating each other, is a far cry from Anaxagoras' views on the indestructibility of matter. It was Greek irreverence towards tradition, Greek dissatisfaction with old answers to perpetually renewable questions, which brought about the change. The process shook the foundations both of religion and of morality. When Xenophanes criticised the religious ideas of his time, he did so from a religious standpoint, replacing beliefs by what he regarded as better beliefs. But the manner of his criticism helped to generate a question, one of the most important questions ever asked in human history, with which intellectuals of the Classical period were (sometimes, perhaps, more deeply than they realised) preoccupied: What is *nature*, which cannot be changed, and what is *convention*, which can?

Are gods really part of the universe in which we find ourselves, or are they a construction of the human imagination, a useful point of reference for organised society? If they exist, do they make laws for us? And if so, do they punish us if we break those laws? Why *should* I do what is called 'right' and abstain from what is called 'wrong'?

### Columns in the Aisle

Cathedrals in which the art of eight centuries can be glimpsed from one spot are not uncommon. The cathedral at Syracuse multiplies that span of time by three. Down the aisles run the columns of a pagan temple of Athena, joined by stonework to form continuous walls, and the square pillars of the nave were created by punching gaps through the inner walls of the temple. This was a holy place long before Christianity, and when a change of deities came to it the work of the pagan builders was not all wasted. In just the same way the Greek tribes themselves, settling in a new area and founding a new city, assimilated and adjusted the religious cults they found there, in preference to sweeping them away as misguided native superstition. Accustomed as they were to differences of cult and ritual and myth between the worship of a given deity in one city-state and the worship of that deity in another city-state twenty miles away, the Greeks applied the same principle to foreign dcities – treating 'Amun', for example, as the Egyptian word for 'Zeus', and treating what the Egyptians said and did in the worship of Amun as the mode of worship which Zeus found acceptable when it was carried out in Egypt. The Persians were less tolerant, sometimes destroying Greek sanctuaries on the grounds that Greek deities were evil spirits. Christianity was the first systematic and uncompromising religion in Greek experience which achieved the power to enforce worship of one God, insisting that all Greek deities were either illusions or devils. At popular level the break was not so sharp, and all over the Mediterranean many local 'heroes' and little local gods underwent a surprisingly smooth transformation into local saints. In Greek popular poetry, all through the Christian centuries, notions of death and the after-life have owed more to pagan than to Christian theology.

The incorporation of the fluted columns of the temple of Athena into the Christian cathedral of Syracuse is a symbol which raises a question: how much of what we commonly regard as Christian is actually an inheritance from pagan times? 'Paganism' does not, and never did, mean 'immorality'. No social creature (and man is a social creature) can survive without a code of practice to which most members of a community, most of the time, conform when their wishes conflict; and that is morality. Each of us is confronted, every day, by the need to compromise between self-interest and the interests of others – or, to put it another way,

43

between the need to survive in competition with other individuals and the need for integration in a set of affectionate and trusting relationships. In Greek drama and in the many law-court speeches which have come down to us from ancient Athens it is generally taken for granted that helpfulness, compassion, generosity and magnanimity are admirable. When we enquire more closely into the circumstances in which these virtues were thought appropriate, some differences between us and the Greeks appear, founded on different definitions of 'community' and different assignation of roles within a community, but that does not affect the similarity of their virtues and ours considered as manifestations of ways of thinking about oneself and others.

In modern English usage 'morality' and 'immorality' are often used with a purely sexual reference. This may be a product of intellectual laziness; it is so much easier to define (e.g.) adultery or sodomy than to define pride or meanness, so much easier to know whether we have exploited a prostitute than to decide whether we have been uncharitable. But there are other reasons too. Most of us are more *interested* in sexual behaviour than in other kinds of behaviour; I recall that when I gave a series of public lectures on Greek views of politics, religion, science and sex the attendance at the lecture on sex was roughly equivalent to the combined attendances at the other lectures. This is no matter for surprise, considering that for most people no activity is more attractive than sexual intercourse, few have as much of it as they would like, and in consequence topics which arouse lust and offer it the satisfaction of fantasy are for many the only unfailingly interesting topics of art, literature and conversation. (Just as well, perhaps; love may determine the quality of life, but the fact that we are alive at all is owed to lust, not love.) Popular enthusiasm for news about Greek sexuality has a touch of (male) wistfulness in it. Men rather like to think that no one had any inhibitions in ancient times, that the golden torch of erotic freedom blazed until it was doused by frustrated monks and sourpuss bishops, and that Eros will come into his own again if only ... But unless I am badly mistaken, Eros *is* coming into his own, and in many ways which would have shocked Greek sensibilities into speechlessness. Greek sexual inhibitions were not all the same as ours; but they were numerous and on occasion remarkably oppressive.

In two striking respects there is no coincidence between theirs and ours: the Greeks thought of gods as enjoying sex, and they thought that homosexual desire and its satisfaction were natural, normal and universal among men and gods alike. In the museum at Olympia, site of the richest and most awe-inspiring sanctuary of Zeus, 'father of gods and men', stands a terracotta statue representing Zeus carrying off Ganymede. The legendary Ganymede was a boy of extraordinary beauty. According to Homer, who composed his work two or three generations before the fashion for overt homosexuality swept through the Greek world and took lasting hold of it, the gods presented Ganymede to Zeus as a cup-bearer. According to post-Homeric poets, Zeus was overcome with desire for Ganymede and carried him off to Olympos. The terracotta at Olympia, contemporary with the majestic sculptures on the great temple of Zeus, shows us Zeus striding off to Olympos purposefully, complacently, with Ganymede tucked under his arm; Ganymede carries a cockerel, a traditional lover's gift from man to boy. To Christians, Jews, and Moslems the notion that God would kidnap a boy and rape him takes a bit of getting used to; what is more, he does it not to consummate a mystic union or symbolise a cosmic principle, but because it is fun. Not so much fun for Ganymede, perhaps, but God's lust is no mean compliment. *Why* the Greeks, alone among civilisations known to us, were not embarrassed at saying, 'I'm desperately in love with a boy', and did not hesitate to elevate the desire of an older for a younger male into an important motif of art and literature, no one really knows. Half the answer may be that they were a very inventive people, and nothing in their tradition suggested to them that enjoying only girls was better than enjoying both girls and boys. Whatever the reason, they did enjoy boys as well as girls from about 600 BC onwards; this is counted by Herodotos among the 'good things of life' which the Persians subsequently learned from the Greeks.

That gods and goddesses (except some resolutely virgin goddesses) should welcome the pleasure afforded by their immortal genitals is wholly in accord with the early Greeks' concept of divinity. The gods are exempt from death and decay, they know much more than we do, and they have much greater power. Like the baron in his castle on the hill, they demand respect, exact tribute, lay down laws and punish offenders. If we are prudent, we do as they say. We may envy them and admire them, and there are occasions when we are overwhelmed with gratitude for what they have done for us, but there are also occasions when they behave in a way which in a fellow-human we should reproach as cruel, ungrateful or unjust. It is commonly assumed nowadays that morality is necessarily derived from religion, and also that if God seems to us morally imperfect, this can only be because our understanding is defective. For the former assumption it is hard to see any excuse, since it is contrary to ordinary experience and observable fact. The latter assumption is excusable, because the nature of moral valuation is notoriously hard to understand; but it is an assumption which many Greeks avoided making.

The 'moralisation' of religion is a process which we can actually trace through the history of Greek literature, and most easily in the development of beliefs about the after-life. In the world of Homer and Hesiod it was believed that the righteous man had some grounds for confidence in divine favour during his lifetime, and the unrighteous some grounds for fearing disaster. After death, the soul of good and bad alike passed a shadowy existence in the underworld, miserably aware that being alive is much nicer than being dead. Only a very few, offspring of the union of gods with women or closely related to such a half-divine person, could hope for eternal bliss, and only the grossest offenders against the gods (by spectacular blasphemy and impiety or attempted rape of a goddess) suffered eternal punishment; perjurers too risked punishment, for to swear falsely by gods involves the divine world in a way which many other kinds of reprehensible behaviour do not.

This is not a very satisfactory set of beliefs. In the first place, we can see for ourselves that the righteous often suffer and the unrighteous often prosper. And secondly, if we pause in the business of life to contemplate a bloodless existence in the shadows for ever and ever, we find it depressing. The emotional need for an assurance of something better was met by the growth of 'mystery' cults, offering preferential treatment in the underworld to those who went through secret rites of initiation during life. The deep emotional need to believe that the universe works *fairly* (a need which we feel above all when our enemies triumph) was met by a doctrine formulated about 600 BC, to the effect that the gods do not always punish unrighteousness promptly but may defer punishment and visit it upon the children or descendants of the sinner. This doctrine has one great strength, that it is not refutable by experience; when a good man suffers, we can say that one of his ancestors must have sinned, and when a sinner prospers, we can comfort ourselves with the assurance that his family will one day suffer.

But *is* that a comfort? Some verses of a poet in the 500s reproach Zeus for the injustice inherent in punishing the innocent for the sins of their forebears.[43] The poet does not reject the doctrine as untrue, nor does he mistrust his own human moral judgement; he simply declares that the divine rule is wrong. Increasing sophistication and preoccupation with the problem of justice and fairness in political structures forced into prominence another emotional need, widespread though by no means universal in human society: the need to believe in *good* gods. Whereas we cannot believe that the baron up on the hill is a good man when we see him with our own eyes do atrocious things from motives which are all too intelligible, we can, if we wish, postulate good gods and explain disaster either as part of a mysterious providential purpose which we cannot expect to understand or as determined by blind Fate and outside the gods' jurisdiction. We have seen how Xenophanes, before 500 BC, chose to form and propagate belief in a new kind of god, and the notion that gods are necessarily good was strongly reinforced by the argument or faith of some (not all) philosophers during the next two centuries.

Equally important was the dissemination of a belief that all of us, without exception, are judged after death and rewarded or punished according to our behaviour on earth. This was a very ancient belief in Egypt, where some elaborate texts prescribe the declarations of innocence expected of the soul (including, incidentally, 'I have not had sexual relations with a boy', which Greeks would not have thought relevant to the fate of their souls). Like the belief in deferred punishment, it is not refutable by experience, because no one comes back to tell us, but it has two advantages: it confines punishment to the sinner who has merited it, lifting a burden from his innocent descendants, and it offers most of us, who do our best and aren't too bad, a better prospect than the peevish fragility of the Homeric underworld. Epitaphs from the 300s BC onwards express the hope that the soul will be conducted to 'the place of the pious' or even to Olympos.

In the classical period many views of the after-life existed together. Some never discarded the Homeric view, while others did not believe that the soul survived the body at all. Some put their faith in initiation, and some simply in virtue. The tragic poets exploited the idea of inherited guilt and deferred punishment, for the myths which they handled lent themselves admirably to dramatic treatment in those terms, but in doing this they may already have been a little out of harmony with common sentiment. Some people believed in an endless chain of reincarnation, though that is never mentioned in epitaphs and probably did not appeal to many. No one was in a position to reject other people's views on the subject as heretical or to defend his own as revealed truth. The religious climate was much more like that of Japan than it was like Christian Europe. Insistence on orthodoxy, dogma and the authority of revelation was imposed by Christianity upon the Greek world. Heaven, Hell and Judgement were a Christian inheritance from Egypt via the Greeks.

Apollo, centaurs and lapiths in the west pediment of the temple of Zeus at Olympia. There is room for controversy about the disposition of some of the figures, but no doubt that Apollo stood at the central point.

# CHAPTER THREE

# Stone, Metal and Flesh

*Olympia*

The first Greek sculpture I ever saw must have been, I suppose, the Elgin Marbles in the British Museum, for I was a Londoner and accustomed from childhood to go to the Museum. It would be nice to think that the Elgin Marbles made a deep impression on me, but the truth is that they made no impression at all. I suppose they looked too much like plaster-casts of themselves in school corridors. But I saw Olympia when I was seventeen, and my response to the great statuary from the pediments of the temple of Zeus, recovered by excavation at the end of the last century and now majestically displayed in the Olympia museum, was strong and immediate. This was Greek sculpture on its home ground, starker and less sophisticated than the Elgin Marbles.

The east pediment is restful, the west pediment tense and violent. As you come into the museum, your eyes are likely to go to the west pediment, and your feet follow. The scene is one of swirling combat between human beings and centaurs. The story is that Peirithoos, king of a tribe called the Lapiths, invited the centaurs to his wedding. Half-animal in form, they were lawless and impulsive by disposition; becoming wildly drunk, they tried to carry off the Lapith women, including the king's bride, and were defeated only after a fearful fight. In the very centre of the pediment is a gigantic figure of the god Apollo, his expression impassive, his right arm extended horizontally.

The sculptors may have been aware that the victory of the Lapiths over the centaurs symbolises the desirable victory of law and civilised behaviour over rape, drunken violence and contempt for the rules of hospitality. They may have intended to convey to us not just that Apollo did on that mythical occasion bless by his unperturbed presence the cause of the Lapiths, but that he is, and will always be, the inspirer and enforcer of rules which distinguish the human from the bestial; that when these rules are broken, the god will arise and his enemies will be scattered. But this symbolism may have been incidental and secondary.

It is the form of the sculpture that delights the spectator today, and perhaps it was in the first place the form that determined the sculptors' choice of subject. Fighting was a good subject for a pediment, because crouching or struggling figures fit naturally between the slope and the base, and fallen figures fit in the corners. When one set of participants in a fight is part horse and part man, and when they are simultaneously grasping furious women and fending off desperate men, a wonderful variety of shapes can be made out of individual combats; a generation after Olympia, the sculptors who made the 'metopes' (exterior panels) for the Parthenon exploited afresh the battle of the centaurs and the Lapiths.

The Apollo of the Olympia pediment is like a great rock rising out of an angry sea, and I am practically certain that my first reaction to him – it – when I saw it in 1937 was admiration for it as a shape among shapes. I felt the same about the labours of Herakles depicted on the metopes, where spare and simple composition is perfectly adapted to the portrayal of tension and rest, and I had admired just that principle of composition in the colour-prints of Hiroshige long before I liked Greek art. When I could look at the Apollo not only as a statue but as a statue *of* somebody, I was crushed by envy. He was endowed with blessings of which I would have welcomed a particle or two for myself: perfect physical strength and shapeliness, and total self-confidence. I thought for many years afterwards that there was no reason why this reaction of mine should be of any interest to anyone, but now I am not so sure; it may be a clue to one aspect of Greek religion. The question, '*Who* was Apollo?', is commonplace and easily answered: he was a son of Zeus by Leto, twin-brother of Artemis, a sort of Crown Prince in Zeus' kingdom, empowered to disclose his father's will to mankind through oracles. The question, '*What* was Apollo?', is less commonplace, and greatly differing kinds of answer have been offered, according to one's inclination in one direction towards anthropology or in the other towards metaphysics. Let me suggest a down-to-earth answer. Apollo was eternally youthful, ineffably beautiful, and invincibly strong; perfectly accomplished in all the arts and sciences, endowed with the foreknowledge which is denied to mankind, effortlessly able to destroy his enemies and protect his friends; he had a lot of girls, and therefore a lot of sons, but no wife; in short, he was what every young male Greek would like to be.

Apollo's greatest sanctuaries were at Delphi and Delos. Olympia belonged to Zeus, and inside the Temple of Zeus was the great seated statue of the god, some forty feet high, made of ivory and gold over a core of wood. It was the work of Pheidias, who also made the ivory and gold statue of Athena in the Parthenon, and one of the most engaging items in the museum at Olympia is a little jug recovered in the excavation of his workshop, bearing his name incised on the bottom. The statue of Zeus has long since vanished; it was taken to Constantinople early in the Christian era, and statues covered with detachable gold do not indefinitely survive financial crises.

But Zeus in marble is the central figure of the east pediment of the temple. When the statuary was all in place on the temple, no one could ever have seen the two pediments simultaneously. In the museum, they face each other and form an extraordinary contrast, for the figures on the east pediment are standing, sitting, kneeling or reclining as if for a group photograph. On either side of the central figures is a four-horse chariot. This is the prelude to a contest, a chariot-race; plainly a momentous race, for otherwise it would not have been portrayed in that place, and perhaps a race disastrous and tragic for one of the contestants, for among the minor figures is an old man seated on the ground, raising his fist to his face in a gesture of apprehension. Interpretation of the group is easy when we know the story.

Once upon a time there was a king of the country round Olympia, and he had a beautiful daughter, whom many young men sought to marry. But the king had been told by an oracle that his son-in-law would be the cause of his death, and he was therefore determined to

An old man seated on the ground: east pediment of the temple of Zeus at Olympia.

have no son-in-law. Whenever a suitor appeared, the king imposed a chariot-race as a condition; he gave the suitor a good start, but then overtook him and killed him. So it went until Pelops arrived from Lydia. One version of the story says that Pelops bribed the king's charioteer to remove an axle-pin from the king's chariot. Another, less brutal version says that Pelops was given magic horses by the god Poseidon. Anyway, he won, and married the girl, and the king died – by a crash, in the one version, or by chagrined suicide, in the other. The myth had a significance far beyond the small region to which it was linked, for the Peloponnese, 'island of Pelops', bears Pelops' name. His sons were Atreus and Thyestes, and Atreus' son was Agamemnon, the focus of so many myths, the great king who died ignominiously in his own house, killed by his wife and her lover. Some Greeks saw a sinister connection between the victory of Pelops and the death of his grandson, for there was a story that Pelops had thought it prudent to kill the king's charioteer; the charioteer, with his dying breath, cursed Pelops, and the grisly misfortunes which beset successive generations of the family stemmed from that curse.

Back now for a last look round at the sculpture of the pediments at Olympia. I said that the old man in the east pediment makes a *gesture* of apprehension. We might imagine that he also wears an *expression* of apprehension. But if we took away the gesture and put him in a context in which he had nothing to be apprehensive about, would we still think so? There is a striking deficiency of emotion in all the faces, and no attempt at individualisation; each sculptor has perfected a recipe for the human face, modified for sex and age but not for personality, for his interest lies in the rest of the body. One marvellous figure in the east pediment has lost its head, and that makes it easy for us to look at it simply as a body. It is a young male, sitting on the ground in a pose perfectly comfortable (for the young) and relaxed, yet ready to push off the ground with palm and sole and be upright in a second. This is the flexibility of flesh represented in stone.

### The Classical Ideal

The skill needed for the portrayal of soft substances in a hard medium was acquired in one exuberant period of artistic innovation, the two generations which preceded the Persian invasion.

Greek sculpture begins in the 'dark age' with small figures in terra-cotta, ivory and bronze. Statues as large as life or larger are known from the middle 600s onwards. Some are free-standing, others in relief as an architectural element of temples, altars and tombs. Their material was usually marble – an abundant material in some parts of the Aegean, especially Attica – or limestone. In its fondness for 'processional' and

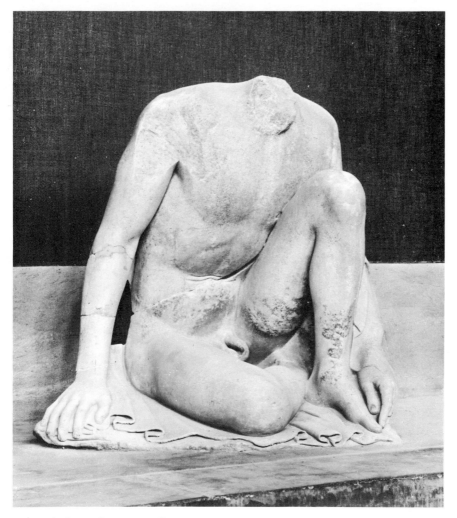

A youth from the east pediment.

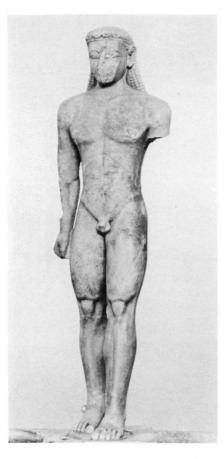

A 'kouros' from Sounion in Attica, made about 600 B C.

*Opposite:* A 'kouros' from the grave of a certain Kroisos, an Athenian or resident in Attica, made in the late 500s B C.

'heraldic' composition, and in other stylistic conventions too, early relief sculpture has something in common with vase-painting of the same period. The earliest free-standing statues might be facetiously described as blocks of stone from which the portions least resembling the human figure have been removed.

The process by which classical sculpture grew and matured is seen most simply by looking at a selection, spaced out in time, of statues of naked young men, known nowadays as *kouroi*, a Greek poetic word for 'boys' or 'youths'. Standing with arms straight down their sides, looking to their front, one foot advanced, the first *kouroi* are a transposition into Greek terms of a sculptural formula which had been used by the Egyptians for two thousand years. One of the most majestic, found at Sounion (the southern tip of Attica) and now in the National Museum in Athens, stands three metres high. Its torso forms an immense slab partially moulded, back and front, into the contours of a human body and incised with a formal pattern which has its point of origin in the musculature of a human body but is far from being a realistic representa-

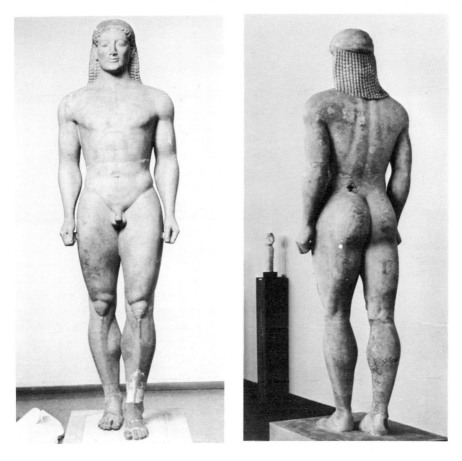

tion of musculature. The ears might be described as an abstract motif in stone suggested by the human ear.

Two generations later another *kouros*, placed as a monument on the grave of a man called Kroisos, displays far greater skill in the moulding of the torso. One generation more, and we stand before a small but remarkable statue in the Acropolis Museum at Athens. Known as the 'Kritian boy', because there is a case for attributing it to the sculptor Kritios, it was probably set up on the Acropolis just before the Persians arrived, and was therefore buried under the debris when the invaders overthrew everything; that would account for the good preservation of its surface. This boy is not standing four-square or marching straight forwards, but wholly relaxed, even minutely wilting, his weight more on one leg than the other. He does not seem to be looking exactly in the direction suggested by the posture of his legs, nor does his torso seem to face exactly the same way as his eyes.

The Kritian boy was made less than a hundred and fifty years after Greek artists first took from the Egyptians the idea of making stone

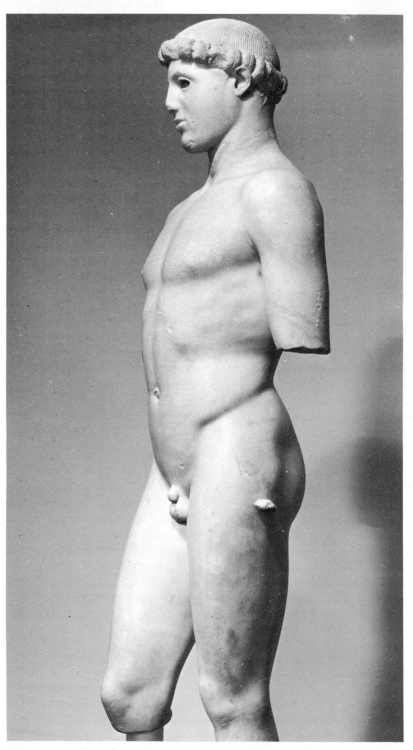

The 'Kritian boy' from the Acropolis at Athens, made at the
beginning of the 400s B.C.

*Left:* An Egyptian statue of about 2500 BC—as long before Kroisos as Michelangelo's David was after. *Right:* An Egyptian statue contemporary with Kroisos. Contrast the similarities of style between these two statues, separated by 2000 years, and the differences between Kroisos and the Kritian boy, separated by some 30–40 years.

statues. He is separated from the Sounion *kouros* by little more than a hundred years, and from Kroisos by about forty. In him Greek art succeeded in doing what it had been trying to do: making stone look like flesh in movement. Considered against the time-scale of the history of art in the ancient world, the progress from stone boy to boy in stone was extraordinarily rapid. The comparison sets before our eyes in a simple and vivid way the greatest single difference between Greek culture and the culture of the ancient Near East. The Egyptians in particular seemed to the Greeks never to have ventured on artistic innovation since the dawn of history; we would put it more cautiously and say that, having formed an idea of the right way to make a statue of a male human at a very early date, they adhered in essentials to that idea from a time before there were Greeks in Greece right down to the time when Egypt was annexed by the Romans.

I am warned by experience that it is very hard to comment on this phenomenon, even in the most diffident way, without antagonising Egyptologists. They rightly point to interesting and important changes observable in the long history of Egyptian sculpture.[44] But when I say that Egyptian sculpture did not change *in essentials*, I am speaking of the level of difference which enables the museum visitor to say, 'That's archaic Greek', 'That's classical Greek', and 'That's Egyptian', not of the level at which the more knowledgeable say, 'That's Fifth Dynasty Egyptian' and 'That's Nineteenth Dynasty'. The Egyptologist is also prompt to assume that the classicist, in praising the boldness and originality of the Greek artists who struck out on their own to create representational sculpture, necessarily believes that by so doing the Greeks brought art out of childhood into maturity. Personally, I don't believe anything of the kind. They gained something important, but they also lost something important – as, I think, the later development of their art was to show.

When you have succeeded in making marble or bronze look just like a human body in rest or movement, with the contours of every bone and muscle skilfully reproduced, people may start looking at the faces of your statues in a new way and making new demands.

One of the most often photographed of all Greek statues is a great bronze which was found in the sea off the east coast of Greece fifty years ago and is now at Athens. It is a naked bearded male, over two metres high, in the act of brandishing (Poseidon, with his trident?) or hurling (Zeus hurling a thunderbolt?). Standing in front of it, I was asked, 'Yes, but where's its *heart*?' Being disinclined to think that a heart can only be a 'bleeding heart', I thought at once of the power-house inside the chest pumping blood with perfect efficiency throughout the immortal body; but, of course, that isn't what the question meant. We have already had occasion to notice the uniformity and impassivity of the faces on sculpture of the great temple of Zeus at Olympia, which is contemporary with the bronze from the sea. The face of the Kritian boy has been described as 'vacant', perhaps a harsh judgement on a face in which the eye-sockets are literally vacant through no fault of the sculptor's (the inlaid material which represented the eyes has perished). Yet it is true that what people miss in much classical sculpture is the beloved imperfection of real faces and the frailty and instability which real expressions betray.

Let us see whether we miss it in the central masterpiece of the classical period, the Parthenon frieze. The Parthenon is a comparatively well documented building, and datable with precision: from fragments of the commissioners' accounts (inscribed on stone for public display), combined with some literary evidence, we know that it was begun in 448 BC and finished by 432. The quantity of sculpture on it was extraordinary, and the frieze, which ran for over 180 metres right round the building, depicted in idealised form the procession which was part of the greatest festival of Athena. In one section of the frieze gods and goddesses are seated in relaxed and dignified conversation. We can identify them as deities by interpreting their relationship to the procession and by using what we know about the attributes of individual deities in Greek literature and elsewhere in Greek art. Without that knowledge, looking at the seated deities as if they were a unique fragment surviving from an age of which we were otherwise wholly ignorant, no one could say with assurance that they must be divine and not human. The first *kouroi* to

Gods and goddesses in the frieze of the Siphnian Treasury at Delphi, about 530 BC (*above*), and in the frieze of the Parthenon at Athens, about 440 BC (*below*). The difference in hair, clothing and pose illustrates the technical development which Greek sculpture underwent in less than a century.

Relief sculpture on the grave of Ktesileos and Theano, foreign
residents at Athens, about 370 B C.

Relief sculpture from Athens, showing a procession of horsemen, about 550 B.C.

be discovered in modern times were in fact taken to be statues of Apollo, but most of them are not. This is one respect in which Greek art is singularly different from that of older cultures. Confronted with a female figure in stone, if she has sixteen tits and a crocodile's head, we know she's not the girl next door; but many a goddess depicted by a Greek sculpture could be just that. Comparison between the deities on the Parthenon and the humans on Athenian grave-reliefs is rewarding. The visual humanisation of deities is analogous to the Greek poet's investment of deities with human passions, a consequence of a highly conscious love of life rather than an unnoticed survival from an age of primitive naïvety.

Its counterpart is the idealisation of humanity. The extraordinary gravity which we see in the faces of the deities in the Parthenon frieze appears also on the faces of the young men riding horses in another part of the frieze. You may shrink from those young men, thinking that they look too like school prefects of the most odious kind, but no one could call those intensely serious faces 'vacant'. Riding frisky stallions without saddles or stirrups, they are totally confident of their ability to do what is required of them, as confident as any one of us would wish to be in their place. This may give us a clue to the understanding of the Greek artist's purpose and his public's expectations – a highly speculative matter, since we have only occasional wisps of aesthetic theory from classical times and therefore have to reconstruct their theory in whatever way we judge most easily reconcilable with all relevant considerations.

It seemed (I suggest) self-evident to the Greek artist that if he was going to the trouble of creating something, it should be better to look at than the ugly people and things, the failures and disappointments, which crowd upon us in our ordinary lives. The business of art was to make good the deficiencies of nature and chance. If, therefore, he had mastered the technique of producing in stone what seemed to him the most beautiful imaginable face, whatever was the point of deliberately producing one less beautiful? And if it was possible to portray things going

*Above and opposite:* Relief sculpture from the Parthenon, rather more than 100 years after the previous picture, of young men riding horses.

perfectly right, why portray them going wrong, even in the least particular? This is the essence of classical idealism; and it explains why each individual artist, having arrived at what he felt to be the right formula for the human face, put the same face on all his figures.

'Self-expression', a term which has no Greek equivalent, would have meant to the Greek artist the freedom to choose and dispose the elements which in combination satisfied the community's demand, or his patron's demand, for a particular theme to fulfil a particular social and religious function. The notion that self-expression is of any value *in itself* was quite alien to the Greeks. If the quality of the self which was being expressed was acknowledged to be high, they would be willing to give it a look or a hearing; but if it expressed itself in a style which was technically slovenly or insufficiently subjected to self-criticism, they would soon lose patience and say, 'Go away, and don't come back until you can express yourself in a way we can respect.'

The public set a high technical standard. It expected each generation of artists to master the techniques of the previous generation and to tackle new problems. When hard material had been made to look like flesh, the next problem was to make it look like hair and fabrics. With what success the sculptors applied themselves to this task can plainly be seen from a comparison between the seated deities in the Parthenon frieze and a similar scene in the frieze of a small rectangular building, the 'Treasury of Siphnos', erected at Delphi eighty years earlier. The

Siphnian frieze is full of vigour, and the formalisation of the hair and clothing contributes positively to that vigour. On the Parthenon, curly hair and the elaborate folds of loose cloth go with the subtler moulding of the bodies and the relaxed posture.

If I confess that the Siphnian frieze both satisfies and stimulates me more than the frieze of the Parthenon, I fear a charge of thoughtless primitivism. The trouble is, I cannot now look at any work of art (nor would I, if I could) as a self-sufficient, self-explanatory object. The Siphnian frieze, at the same moment as I respond to its sheer zest, makes me think in historical terms of the exciting technical problems which the Greek sculptors were going on to solve; and it is *their* experience, not our reactions to their work, which engages my interest and excites my imagination. The Parthenon frieze, the consummation of their involvement with technique, makes me ask, again thinking historically while I look, 'And what *then*?' Because there is an answer to that question, and I have some inkling of the answer, I feel the breeze dropping and the afternoon growing sultry.

### Classicism in the Arts

The first two hundred years of Greek sculpture, from the middle 600s BC down to the Parthenon, were distinguished by innovation and a radical departure from that conception of sculpture as an art-form which was entertained by older civilisations. We might have expected that at some point during the following two hundred years – and to give it a better chance, let us double that and say the following four hundred years, from the Parthenon down to the completion of Rome's supremacy over the Mediterranean basin – we should find the same spirit of artistic innovation at work, the same readiness to take off in a new direction. But that is not what we find.

Now, just as the Egyptologist bristles when he suspects that a classicist is ignorantly and arrogantly dismissing Egyptian art as primitive or immature, so historians and connoisseurs of later Greek art are saddened and angered by treatment of that art as decadent or degenerate. They are quite right; and to move the frontier between 'classical' and 'late' so far back as to discern the first tinge of decadence in the generation immediately after the Parthenon, so condemning the most famous works of the 300s, could fairly be treated as the product of nothing more interesting than a desire to shock. Different people mean different things by 'decadent' (or 'degenerate'), and I myself will call no art such names unless it is manifestly *perfunctory* – unless, that is, we can see that the artist is no longer concentrating his imagination and intelligence on his work and exulting in his skill. 'Perfunctory' is just what later Greek art is *not*.

The late-archaic and early-classical Greek artist embraced with all his energies and skill the problem of making materials which are hard, solid, heavy and enduring represent what is soft, light, fluid, quick and momentary. That is what artists went on doing for the rest of the classical period and thereafter, with increasing skill and refinement. Standing and seated figures relax gracefully, caught in a moment of leisurely and confident movement. Figures in the tension of conflict strain and writhe. Faces are stone made vulnerable in grief, passion or reflection. Cloaks and tunics whisk as people fight and die. Delicate fabrics billow in the breeze as deities sail through the air, alight, and take off.

Greek artists have left us no writings about their art, so that we have no direct evidence about what they wished to do or thought they were doing, but everything that is said about art in Greek literature shows that meticulously realistic representation was admired. One modern art-historian, a lover of the later Greek artists, speaks of their work in Greek terms,[45] for example, 'We almost feel the perspiration or the oil on the skin', or 'We can hear the crackle of flames and screams of agony'.

Sometimes, in certain genres, the later sculptor breaks free of one aesthetic restriction which his predecessors had nearly always observed: the persons he portrays are not all awe-inspiring or enviable for their beauty, strength or dignity. At long last, children look like children, not like pygmies. The bitterness and stringiness of old age, the brutality of a

A portion of the battle between gods and giants depicted on the great altar at Pergamon in Asia Minor, about 160 BC.

massive physique, are expressed in stone and metal.

This willingness to enlarge the functions of realism had one rewarding consequence which I do not think acquaintance with the art of the classical period would have led us to predict: individual portraiture. The idea of portraiture was not unknown to the classical artists, but it was subordinated to idealisation. Relief sculpture on tombs, for example, depicted people not as they were but as it was assumed they would have liked to be; or one could say, the artist translated into visual terms an ideal relationship of which actual human relationships, each with a precise location in time and space, are necessarily imperfect instances. Nevertheless, the artist's interest in the unique individual as a subject for reproduction in stone or bronze edged its way in with increasing boldness as the 300s passed. It comes to life most vividly in the portraits of the men of Greek and Macedonian ancestry who ruled the kingdoms of the Near East into which Alexander's great empire broke up. Their profiles on their coins are highly individual: sombre, intense, or quirky. A sculptured head of Euthydemos I of Bactria, who reigned in the last third of the 200s, is the most memorable surviving example of the genre. These heavy features, soured by experience yet in no way incompatible with candour, tenderness and self-criticism, may or may not be a good likeness of Euthydemos – how can we know? – but their affinity with his head on the coins which he issued at least assures us that the sculptor was not committing a secret act of hostility against the king.

Why did those kings like to proclaim their sweaty distance from divinity? If an explanation must be sought in the beliefs and values of

Portrait-head of Euthydemos I of Bactria, about 200 BC.

their time, we may remember that one of the many strands of philosophical thinking which had their origin in Socrates was contemptuous
of human ambition, insistent on the transitory and illusory nature of
power and wealth, on the simplicity of the needs common to all men by
virtue of their humanity, and on the brevity and fragility of human life.
To this sentiment a reminder that kings could be ugly and tired and
sick was a recognition of reality, an integration of oneself into the world.
But, of course, there are other kinds of explanation. Perhaps the kings
liked to be identified at once as individuals, especially on their coins.

1  A view southward from the citadel of Mycenae. The conical hill in the distance
on the right is the citadel of Argos; Tiryns, a low flat mound, is ten miles
away and not easily discerned in this (or any) picture.

2  The remains of a helmet dedicated to Zeus at Olympia by
Miltiades. Miltiades was one of the Athenian generals at
Marathon, and tradition gave him the credit for Athens' victory.
Those who are sure they cannot read Greek may none the less
decipher Miltiades' name on the helmet; the script and spelling
are those used by the Athenians in the early 400s BC.

3 Acrocorinth, now crowned by the ruins of Turkish fortifications, towers above the ancient city of Corinth, where the narrow Isthmus joins the Peloponnese to the rest of Greece.

4 *Opposite, above:* This view of Syracuse shows Ortygia, the oldest part of the city, joined to the mainland by a bridge. The sea in the left half of the picture is the north-east quarter of the Great Harbour. The water to the right of Ortygia is open sea.

5 The bed of the river now called Assinaro, photographed
from the bridge by which the coastal road crosses it (hence
the shadow). It is almost certain that it is rightly named
after the ancient Assinaros, where the Athenians in retreat
from Syracuse were finally overcome, but the identification
is not wholly free from difficulties; nor is any alternative
identification.

6 Fossil sea-shells embedded in limestone in a Syracuse quarry. Such fossils provoked in Xenophanes speculation about the past.

7 *Left:* These fluted columns in the cathedral at Syracuse started life as columns of the pagan temple of Athena, on exactly the spot where they still stand.

8 *Opposite:* Zeus, captivated by the beauty of Ganymede, carries him off to Olympia. The terracotta statue was made about 470 B C.

9 Zeus hurling a thunderbolt, Poseidon wielding his trident, or ...? This great bronze, made about 460 BC, was recovered from the bottom of the sea off the east coast of Greece earlier this century.

10 Odysseus and his companions plunge the stake into the Cyclops' eye; Attic vase-painting, about 650 B C.

11 *Below:* The same scene depicted by a Peloponnesian vase-painter, about the same date. This painter, unlike his Athenian contemporary, feels no compulsion to fill up blank space with decorative motifs.

12 A Minoan jug from Phaistos in Crete about 1500 BC.

14 The most majestic of surviving Attic Geometric vessels, about 750 BC.

13 From the 'Dark Age': a sub-Mycenaean vessel, from a grave at Athens, made about 1100 BC.

15 Priam, white-haired, brings Achilles a ransom for the body of Hektor. The body lies under Achilles' couch. Immediately behind Priam, the god Hermes, who has escorted him through the night to the Greek camp, waves him farewell.

17 Orestes stabs Aigisthos. Klytaimestra advances upon him, swinging an axe, but Agamemnon's old herald restrains her. This Attic vase was made a few years before 500 B C, probably inspired by the lyric poet Stesikhoros' treatment of the myth.

16 *Opposite:* The centre panel of this bronze relief from Olympia—made about 570 B C, well over a century before the *Oresteia*—is almost certainly a portrayal of Orestes killing Klytaimestra.

18 Thetis and the Nereids mourn the dead Achilles. Contrast this Corinthian vase (about 570 BC) with the schematised mourners and corpse of plate 14.

19 Tydeus kills Ismene ('Hysmena'), while her lover escapes; you can read their names once you know that the early Corinthian script was normally written from right to left.

Perhaps also the drive towards absolutely realistic portraiture came from within the visual arts themselves, as the last province waiting to be conquered by technical skill, and was welcomed by patrons of the arts on terms dictated by good taste.

Whatever the reason, it was in fact the last conquest. By the end of the pre-Christian era Greek art had exploited its own virtuosity to the finish, and it did not know where to go next. So much had gone marvellously right; but when art reaches a point beyond which it ceases to develop new ideas, something has gone badly wrong. In the case of later Greek art, what went wrong (in my opinion) was that the Greek artist was unable to take his mind off the things and events he wanted to reproduce in recalcitrant material and turn it towards the material itself, asking what forms were positively prompted by that material.

'Unable' is perhaps a question-begging word; we can see what people in the past did or didn't do, but we should be wary of saying what they could or couldn't. At least we can see an analogy between the visual arts and literature from the late 300s B C onwards, and if we can explain why literature developed as it did we may find the explanation applicable also to the visual arts.

In the classical period Athens became the cultural centre of the Greek world. Athenian drama, the greatest achievement of the 400s, was admired and disseminated. Athenian prose literature, thanks to the genius of writers like Thucydides, Plato and Demosthenes, established the dialect of Athens, Attic Greek, as the appropriate medium for prose. The universal treatment of Athenian literature as a model brought with it a tendency to absorb and imitate the Athenian spirit. But in that spirit there was a streak of corrosion; for the disastrous defeat of Athens in the Peloponnesian War deprived her of the dominant position of power and wealth which she had enjoyed for so long during the 400s, and Athenians of the 300s felt themselves unequal to their forefathers. This feeling began to generate the notion that the days of their forefathers constituted a model which could be to some degree imitated but could not be surpassed; a notion which is not good for the arts. It is a striking fact that when Euripides and Sophokles were dead (in 406 and 405 respectively) the steam began to go out of tragedy; within thirty years we find that revivals of their plays begin to appear in place of new tragedies at the dramatic festivals, and about 330 B C steps were taken to ensure the preservation of an 'authentic', 'official' text of Aeschylus, Sophokles and Euripides, our first precise evidence of the formation of a classical canon of Greek tragedy. This nostalgic 'classicism' was very strongly reinforced by the subjection of the Greek city-states to the Macedonian monarchy. The Greeks did not conclude (as they might have done) that inbuilt characteristics of their own culture had led them into this predicament, but rather that they had not been valiant, virtuous and wise enough within the framework of their own system of values. Inheriting as they did traditions of a heroic age, a Golden Age, they could not readily admit that their remoter ancestors had been wrong; they felt instead that they themselves had failed to live up to the standards of those ancestors.

After the end of the 300s new developments in literature were – well, I am tempted to say 'comparatively minor', but let me at least say, of such a kind that not everyone instantly agrees that they were of major significance, in the sense that Aeschylus, Herodotos, Thucydides and the Socratic dialogues of Plato represent innovations of major significance. A tendency to classicism set in, conscious and explicit from the last pre-Christian century onwards, not adequately balanced by the development of new literary forms; serious prose drama, for example, the serious novel, serious poetry in vernacular idiom, all stayed in the womb of Europe.

The visual arts differed from literature in so far as few artists declared the supremacy of the classical era and deplored their own capacity to rival it. They did, however, refrain from questioning the unique validity of representational realism. So in the end, having begun its long history by irreverent treatment of tradition, Greek art turned its own achievements into a tradition which demanded and received reverence.

# CHAPTER FOUR

# Poetry and Painting

## The One-eyed Giant

In the museum at Eleusis stands a great storage-jar, four and a half feet high, decorated with crude and lively scenes. On the neck of the vessel three men exert all their strength to thrust a stake into the eye of a giant. The giant, roaring in agony, clutches with one hand at the stake. This vessel was made in Attica about 650 BC. Across in the Peloponnese, at Argos, is a fragment of the same date which displays the same cruel scene: the men thrusting the stake, the giant clutching at it, blood pouring down his face.

The vase-painters have illustrated one of the oldest and most wide-spread stories in the world; some know it as one of the adventures of Sinbad the Sailor, but for the Greeks it was an adventure of Odysseus, experienced on his long and hazardous journey back home from the Trojan War. The story is told in Book Nine of Homer's *Odyssey*. Rounding the southern tip of the Peloponnese, heading for Ithake ('Ithaca'), his native island, Odysseus is driven off course by strong winds. For nine days he and his companions are at the mercy of wind and tide; and when they land on the tenth day in the country of the Lotus-eaters, we find that they are no longer in Greek waters but in a fairyland of marvels and monsters. The story, that is to say, was shaped at a time when Italy, Sicily and North Africa were not a stable part of the Greeks' picture of the world.

From the Lotus-eaters Odysseus comes to the land of the Cyclopses, one-eyed giants who live in caves, each by himself, tending his flocks. They enter the cave of the Cyclops Polyphemos, hoping for the respect and hospitality which the Greeks regarded as a duty imposed by Zeus. But the Cyclopses are a lawless people. Polyphemos blocks the mouth of the cave with a gigantic rock, eats two of Odysseus' companions raw, and goes to sleep. It is useless to kill him while he sleeps, for they would never be able to move the rock at the mouth of the cave and get away. Odysseus, however, is the most resourceful of heroes and, while the

Cyclops is out with his flocks the next day, he thinks of a plan. He finds a great staff of olive-wood in the cave, sharpens it to a point, hardens it in the fire, and hides it under the sheep-dung on the floor of the cave. The Cyclops returns and eats two more men. Odysseus produces a splendid wine, a gift from a priest at his first port of call on the journey from Troy, and the Cyclops drinks deeply of this wine. 'Tell me your name,' he says to Odysseus, 'and I'll make you a gift of great value, in return for your wine.' Odysseus says that his name is 'Nobody'. 'All right,' says the Cyclops with a coarse laugh, 'I'll eat Nobody last!' So saying, he collapses into drunken sleep. Stealthily, Odysseus and his men draw the sharpened stake of olive-wood from under the dung.

> Now, by the gods, I drove my big hand spike
> deep in the embers, charring it again,
> and cheered my men along with battle talk
> to keep their courage up; no quitting now.
> The pike of olive, green though it had been,
> reddened and glowed as if about to catch.
> I drew it from the coals, and my four fellows
> gave me a hand, lugging it near the Cyclops
> as more than natural force nerved them; straight
> forward they sprinted, lifted it and rammed it
> deep in his crater eye, and I leaned on it,
> turning it as a shipwright turns a drill
> in planking, having men below to swing
> the two-handled strap that spins it in the groove.
> So with our brand we bored that great eye-socket,
> while blood ran out around the red-hot bar.
> Eyelid and lash were seared; the pierced ball
> hissed broiling, and the roots popped.
>                                    In a smithy
> one sees a white-hot axehead or an adze
> plunged and wrung in a cold tub, screeching steam –
> the way they make soft iron hale and hard;
> just so that eyeball hissed around the spike.
> The Cyclops bellowed and the rock roared round him,
> and we fell back in fear. Clawing his face,
> he tugged the bloody spike out of his eye,
> threw it away, and his wild hands went groping;
> then he set up a howl for Cyclopes
> who lived in caves in windy peaks nearby.
> Some heard him; and they came by divers ways
> to clump around outside and call:
>                                    'What ails you,
> Polyphemos? Why do you cry so sore
> in the starry night? You will not let us sleep.

Sure no man's driving off your flock? No man
has tricked you, ruined you?'
                                          Out of the cave
the mammoth Polyphemos roared in answer:
'Nohbdy, Nohbdy's tricked me, Nohbdy's ruined me!'
To this rough shout they made a sage reply:
'Ah well, if nobody has played you foul
there in your lonely bed, we are no use in pain
given by great Zeus. Let it be your father,
Poseidon Lord, to whom you pray.'
                                          So saying
they trailed away. And I was filled with laughter
to see how like a charm the name deceived them.
Now Cyclops, wheezing as the pain came on him,
fumbled to wrench away the great doorstone
and squatted in the breach with arms thrown wide
for any silly beast or man who bolted –
hoping somehow I might be such a fool.
But I kept thinking how to win the game;
death sat there huge; how could we slip away?
I drew on all my wits, and ran through tactics,
reasoning as a man will for dear life,
until a trick came – and it pleased me well.
The Cyclops' rams were handsome, fat with heavy
fleeces, a dark violet.
                                          Three abreast
I tied them silently together, twining
cords of willow from the ogre's bed;
then slung a man under each middle one
to ride there safely, shielded left and right.
So three sheep could convey each man. I took
the woolliest ram, the choicest of the flock,
and hung myself under his belly,
pulled up tight, with fingers twisted deep
in sheepskin ringlets for an iron grip.
So, breathing hard, we waited until morning.

When Dawn spread out her finger tips of rose,
the rams began to stir, moving for pasture,
and peals of bleating echoed round the pens
where dams with udders full called for a milking.
Blinded, and sick with pain from his head wound,
the master stroked each ram, then let it pass,
but my men riding on the pectoral fleece
the giant's blind hands blundering never found.[46]

The great ram who is burdened with Odysseus walks with faltering steps.
The giant perceives this by touch; but the poet, who could have created

71

a moment of crude suspense by making suspicion flare up in the giant's mind, chooses instead to create pathos. The giant speaks to the ram lovingly, asking him if he is grieving for his master's fate. The dumb beast plods on, bearing Odysseus to safety.

We are made to feel sorry for the Cyclops; and it is hard not to flinch, identifying ourselves with an unsuspecting fellow-creature, when we think of the hot stake plunging into his eye. But what should people do when they are imprisoned by a giant who eats two of them every day? Recommend him to seek help from a counsellor? That Homer should enable us to share *both* in the suffering of the Cyclops *and* in the exultation of Odysseus is characteristic of Greek poetry. Failure to perceive this consistent characteristic has often led to misunderstandings of Greek attitudes to war: on the one hand, to vilification of a warrior-culture, and on the other, to glorification of what appear to be pacifist sentiments. The Greeks were well aware that to be maimed or starved or widowed is horrible, *and* that to risk death and pain in protecting others is noble, *and* that to come through such a risk victorious is joyful. Laboriously, fitfully, they became aware that it is barbarous to make war on the innocent merely to increase one's own power and wealth, or to kill thousands to avenge a trivial wrong. Until our own time, few nations in the last two thousand years appear to have had a firm grasp of this principle.

### The Ransoming of Hektor

Homer's *Iliad* tells the story of an event in the tenth and last year of the Trojan War. Achilles, son of a mortal man and a goddess, commander of a tribe from Thessaly, a young warrior of incomparable speed, ferocity and fighting skill, quarrels with Agamemnon, the commander of the Greek host at Troy, and refuses to fight. The Greeks in consequence are hard pressed, and when the situation has become desperate Patroklos, Achilles' companion, persuades Achilles to let him enter the battle. He borrows Achilles' arms and armour, and the tide is turned for a while; but he falls victim to Hektor, son of the Trojan king Priam. The death of Patroklos afflicts Achilles with terrible grief, shame and anger. He becomes reconciled to Agamemnon; his goddess-mother gets him new armour, made by the god Hephaistos; and after driving the Trojans before him 'like frightened deer' he kills Hektor.

But his grief for Patroklos and hatred for the man who killed Patroklos are unassuageable. He drags Hektor's body behind his chariot around the grave of Patroklos, day after day, with no thought of accepting a ransom for it and returning it to Troy for a funeral. The gods look down from Olympos and debate whether they should intervene. Apollo speaks first:

'How heartless and how malevolent you are!
Did Hektor never make burnt offering
of bulls' thigh-bones to you, and unflawed goats?
Even in death you would not stir to save him
for his dear wife to see, and for his mother,
his child, his father Priam, and his men:
they'd burn the corpse at once and give him burial.
Murderous Achilles has your willing help,
a man who shows no decency, implacable,
barbarous in his ways as a wild lion
whose power and intrepid heart
sway him to raid the flocks of men for meat.
The man has lost all mercy;
he has no shame – that gift that hinders mortals
but helps them too. A sane one may endure
an even dearer loss: a blood-brother,
a son, and yet, by heaven, having grieved
and passed through mourning, he will let it go.
The fates have given patient hearts to men –
not this one: first he took Prince Hektor's life,
and now he drags the body, lashed to his car,
around the barrow of his friend, performing
something neither nobler in report
nor better in itself. Let him take care,
or, brave as he is, we gods will turn against him,
seeing him outrage the insensate earth!'[47]

Apollo uses two different pleas. One is reproach to the gods for ingratitude: Hektor has punctiliously and generously sacrificed to them, and now in return they should protect his body against maltreatment. The other plea is moral and aesthetic: Achilles is unreasonable in his extravagant grief, shameless, cruel, merciless. Hera retorts:

'Lord of the silver bow, your words would be
acceptable if one had a mind to honour
Hektor and Achilles equally.
But Hektor suckled at a woman's breast,
Achilles is the first-born of a goddess –
one I nursed myself. I reared her, gave her
to Peleus, a strong man whom the gods loved.
All of you were present at their wedding –
you too, friend of the base, for ever slippery,
came with your harp and dined there!'[48]

In other words: 'Achilles is one of *us*!' Now, even if Hera were a real person and Homer the accurate reporter of a real event, we could still not ask, 'Did Hera believe that Achilles' relationship to the gods should take precedence over all other considerations?', for her motive (according to Homer) was hatred of Troy. Because the Judgement of Paris, another of Priam's sons, had gone against her, she will not allow Troy to receive any comfort, and she uses, as a means to an end (but with the genuine emotion engendered by bias), whatever arguments she feels are most likely to deter the gods from intervention. So does Apollo. Homer, like the Greek dramatists after him, makes his characters say what those characters would be likely to say in those circumstances.

Apollo's appeal to the gratitude of the gods prevails with Zeus: Hektor had indeed never failed to honour him in sacrifice and ritual. So Zeus sends Iris, the rainbow, on an errand: first she must go to Achilles' mother Thetis, who will convey Zeus' wishes to Achilles, and then on to Priam, to tell him to go through the night to the Greek camp and offer a rich ransom to Achilles for Hektor's body.

Priam prepares to go. His queen Hecuba reproaches him for his folly in risking his life by going into the presence of the savage Achilles, into whose liver, she says, she would like to sink her teeth. Priam agrees that if he had been told by a priest or a seer to offer Achilles a ransom, he would have refused; but he has seen Iris with his own eyes, and cannot reject a command of Zeus delivered by a goddess. Off he goes, with his herald in attendance and a cart laden with rich presents. The god Hermes meets them in the dark and escorts them through the Greek lines, casting a magic sleep upon the sentries, to the very hut where Achilles and his friends have just finished their evening meal. Before anyone can notice him or stop him, Priam clasps the knees of Achilles in a gesture of supplication and kisses the deadly hands that had killed so many of his sons, crying:

> 'Remember your own father,
> Achilles, in your godlike youth: his years,
> like mine, are many, and he stands upon
> the fearful doorstep of old age. He too
> is hard pressed, it may be, by those around him,
> there being no one able to defend him
> from bane of war and ruin. Ah, but he
> may nonetheless hear news of you alive,
> and so with glad heart hope through all his days
> for sight of his dear son, come back from Troy,
> while I have deathly fortune. Noble sons
> I fathered here, but scarce one man is left me.
> Fifty I had when the Akhaians came,
> nineteen out of a single belly, others
> born of attendant women. Most are gone.
> Raging Ares cut their knees from under them.
> And he who stood alone among them all,
> their champion, and Troy's, ten days ago

you killed him, fighting for his land, my prince,
Hektor.
      It is for him that I have come
among these ships, to beg him back from you,
and I bring ransom without stint. Achilles,
be reverent toward the great gods! And take
pity on me, remember your own father.
Think me more pitiful by far, since I
have brought myself to do what no man else
has done before – to lift to my lips the hand
of one who killed my son.'
      Now in Achilles
the evocation of his father stirred
new longing, and an ache of grief. He lifted
the old man's hand and gently put him by.
Then both were overborne as they remembered:
the old king huddled at Achilles' feet
wept, and wept for Hektor, killer of men,
while great Achilles wept for his own father,
and for Patroklos once again: and sobbing
filled the room.[49]

A poet telling the story of Hektor, Priam and Achilles *could* leave the gods out of it. He could make the ransoming of the body a bold and desperate idea on Priam's part, sustained by faith in the power of an appeal for compassion; and Achilles would suddenly be enlightened, converted, moved to repentance and compassion by seeing in the unhappy Priam someone just like his own aged father. Or again, the poet could lay all the responsibility for events upon the gods; Achilles would be inwardly unrelenting, but would none the less accept the ransom and give up the body because his mother has brought him the command of Zeus, and only a fool fights against Zeus.

When I say 'a poet' I am speaking partly in hypothetical terms, for no poet living at Homer's time and place could in fact have left out the gods; the early Greeks treated the weather, illness, unforeseeable turns of events, sudden thoughts and changes of feeling, as powerful external forces acting upon man, and it was precisely the interventions and comings and goings of gods and goddesses 'before our very eyes' which invested the heroic age, the subject of poetry, with its magic and splendour. But there is a sense in which a poet of Homer's time and place *need* not have portrayed Achilles as moved to tears by Priam's plight. Homer chose to do it, and in doing it he created a dramatic scene of memorable pathos, leaving for ever unanswerable the question, '*Why* did Achilles give up the body – prudent obedience to Zeus, or repentance and compassion?'

This is just the kind of question which it is interesting to ask, and impossible to answer, in respect of situations in Greek tragedy. The death of Patroklos, the death of Hektor and the ransoming of the body formed the theme of a set of plays by Aeschylus, known to us now only from a few fragments, quotations and references. We know that Aeschylus, in conformity with the taste of his day, departed from Homer in making Patroklos younger than Achilles and the object of homosexual passion on the part of the latter, but we do not know how he presented the interplay of divine intervention and human response.

When Aeschylus wrote those plays Athenian vase-painters had already included the arrival of Priam in Achilles' hut among the host of subjects which they drew from the early poets. These pictures do not exactly 'illustrate' Homer, because they were made some two hundred years after Homer, but they do display a mixture of the way in which the Greeks around 500 BC visualised Homeric scenes and the way in which the vase-painters, operating within the artistic conventions imposed by their medium and technique, laid out such scenes. A vase now in Munich brings out this point. Achilles (unlike heroes in Homer) lies on a couch, the food on a little table beside him, Hektor's corpse stowed under the couch. Achilles is fully bearded; the vase belongs to a time at which a tendency to make young heroes and youthful gods unbearded is apparent but not yet universal. Priam, white-haired, approaches him with a gesture, and behind Priam come attendants with horses and gifts (not just the solitary herald and the cartful of treasures of the Homeric story). One attendant is wearing Asiatic dress, for whereas in Homer there is no cultural or linguistic difference between Greeks and Trojans, later times increasingly regarded the Trojan War as a conflict between Europe and Asia, Greeks and 'barbarians'. This is a shift of attitude, between Homer and the Greeks' view of Homer, at a comparatively superficial level. A deeper shift of attitude appears when they turn their minds to the cause of the Trojan War, the theft of Helen, wife of Agamemnon's brother, Menelaos, by Paris, the son of Priam. 'All that', they asked themselves, 'for one man's wife?', and sought other explanations and justifications: the inscrutable will of Zeus, or the benefit conferred upon the Greeks by the eternal examples of valour which the war provided.

### Colour and Space

At first sight the vase-paintings which depict Odysseus and the Cyclops look like children's work. They reflect the absorption of the painter in his task, his natural flair for expressive movement – and his indifference to representational accuracy, save for an endearing preoccupation, on the part of the Argive painter, with kneecaps.

By contrast, the painter of Priam's arrival in Achilles' hut displays an effortless competence in the representation of stance and movement, equally fluid whether it is vigorous or relaxed. This painter is by no means a solitary genius, but one of very many who produced the thousands of (mainly Corinthian and Attic) 'black-figure' and (Attic and South Italian) 'red-figure' vases which we possess. He is separated from the Cyclops vases by a century and a half. Obviously a lot happened to Greek painting during that time, and what happened is one more illustration of the pace and scope of Greek innovation and experiment.

Let us go back to the beginning, which in the case of vase-painting in Greece and the Aegean means the period 2500–2000 BC, when simple patterns of black lines first appear as an alternative to an older tradition of incised patterns or plain surfaces. During 2000–1500 the Minoans made and decorated much pottery of great elegance and refinement; their favoured motifs were vegetable (flowers, grasses, palm-trees) and marine (seaweed, shells and squids). The style of Mycenaean pottery was derived from that, but the Mycenaeans showed greater fondness for human figures, horses, bulls and birds, which they almost always translated into formal patterns, as if they were less interested in an animal than in the abstract forms which the shape of the animal suggested. This formalisation was intensified and simplified as Mycenaean civilisation declined, until in what is called 'Sub-Mycenaean' art (roughly from 1150 to 1000 BC) ingredients which had once been recognisable representations of creatures had turned into simple abstract groupings of lines and spots.

Slowly, a new concept of decoration emerged: very slowly indeed at first, for the decline, the trough and the upward climb occupy the best part of three and a half centuries, from 1150 to 800 BC. Throughout this period there was no lack of potters who had a wonderful eye for vases of clean, spare, elegant shape. Spareness of decoration too can be a great virtue, but in these Greek vases it does not reflect, as the shape of the vessel does, the judgement of mature craftsmen. It seems somehow crude and perfunctory, as if mere convention demanded that pottery should not go naked on the market-place. Yet these rough wavy lines and bands and naïve motifs are a thread which links the art of the Minoans and Mycenaeans to the art of Homer's time. One might compare them to a tuber surviving a very long winter, save that the plant which sprouted from them in the spring of the late 800s did not run true to species: it was a new plant altogether. What happened was that the artist now built up from simple elements great abstract patterns to cover the whole surface of the vessel: triangles, diamonds, meanders, concentric arcs, arrayed in bands, one band separated from the next by sets of parallel lines. The artist exercises a judgement more like an architect's than a painter's: how big an area to cover with a given motif, where to impose the boundary-lines, when to repeat a motif. This is 'Geometric' art, arising out of 'Sub-Mycenaean' through 'Proto-Geometric'.

77

On this Assyrian relief of about 650 BC the movement of an angry lion is accurately observed and expressed. The artist was working in a genre, the royal hunting scene, with over 200 years of tradition behind it; the portrayal of humans changed little during that time, but the animals gained in vitality.

From the beginning, the Geometric vase-painter admitted representational painting in small doses, subordinating it firmly to his abstract scheme. A great vase in the National Museum at Athens, a storage-jar in form (a metre and a half high) but actually made as a work of art to mark a tomb, illustrates the principle very clearly. Round the middle of the neck, bounded by parallel lines above and below, is a row of deer feeding; each is identical with its neighbour, a deer-shaped motif rather than a picture of a deer. On the shoulder of the vessel, between the handles, is a funeral scene, showing the dead man on his bier surrounded by mourners. These humans are more formalised than the deer, each having a torso like an inverted triangle perched on a pair of legs and surmounted by a featureless head.

When that vessel was made, the art of epic poetry was already mature. It may well be that Homer was already born; he was certainly active and famous as a poet before the Cyclops vases were made. It is worth asking ourselves the question: if we had Homer but no Greek art at all, what should we have imagined the art of his time to be like? Or conversely, if we had plenty of Greek art but no Greek literature at all, what sort of literature should we have imagined as contemporary with the vase-painting of the period 750–650 BC? The difficulty of arriving at the truth would be compounded if our point of comparison were the art and literature of the Babylonians and Assyrians during that same period,

In this Greek vase-painting of about 700 BC the lion is crude and
schematic.

so that we were comparing their skilled and sophisticated relief sculpture
with primitive Greek vase-painting, or their narrative poetry (I refrain
from derogatory adjectives; read it and judge) with Greek epic. The
truth is, of course, that we should be very unwise to infer anything about
any art-form in any culture from other art-forms in that culture. Great
novels can coexist with wretched music, or great operas with footling
plays. A culture that invests equal energy in all art-forms is a rarity; and
even if the investment is equal, every art-form strives after autonomy,
sometimes with such success that it is hard to discern tendencies common
to all the arts in the same place and time. Inevitably, analogies between
the architecture of a Greek epic and the architecture of a big geometric
vase have been sought, for there they both are, and the search for
analogies and relationships is irresistible; but what it finds may be
fanciful.

The band of deer and the funeral panel on the great Geometric vase
in Athens are 'growth-points' of the utmost importance for the development of the art of vase-painting. We can see a tiny step towards representational painting taken in a vase of similar date, now in Munich: a
row of birds runs round the bottom, at first sight identical – but one bird,
just one, raises its head while all the others feed, and that detail turns a
row of bird-like shapes into a picture of a flock of birds feeding.

Eventually the pictorial panel which on the Athens vase is so formalised

The raising of one bird's head on the lowest band of this Geometric vase turns a decorative pattern into a picture.

and inset in a solid wall of abstract patterns grows until it becomes the focus of interest, while the abstract decoration, pushed up to the neck of the vessel and down to its foot, becomes a picture-frame. There is an illuminating contrast between the funeral panel on the Attic Geometric vase and a depiction of Thetis and the Nereids mourning for Achilles on a Corinthian vase made nearly two hundred years later. The layout of the figures is still 'processional', but they are now real female figures, and differentiated in their clothing and the movement of their arms. A processional or heraldic disposition of figures remains very common in the 600s, but narrative scenes come to predominate. One such scene, on a Corinthian vase in the Louvre, throws an interesting light on a corner of a well-known myth. Readers of Sophokles' *Antigone*, in which Antigone dies because she defies the king's order not to give her brother the rites of burial, sometimes wonder what happened to her sister Ismene, who is absolved of complicity. Thanks to an ancient commentator, we know that according to the early poet Mimnermos she was married to Tydeus, son of Diomede, and he killed her when she had committed adultery with Theoklymenos. The Louvre vase shows us a man killing a woman, who lies in a bed, while another (naked) man flees. The painter has labelled the figures: the woman is 'Hysmena', her killer 'Tydeus' and her defeated lover 'Periklymenos'. It is a simple, vigorous scene, enhanced by an uncommon element of expressionism: it is a normal convention of this period of vase-painting that men should be painted black and women white, but the painter has also shown the adulterer – worsted and put to flight – as white.

The labelling of characters with their names was common down to the late 500s, and no doubt reflects the painter's anxiety that we should be in no doubt about the identity of the scene depicted. But it also reflects his unwillingness to leave empty spaces. Look back at the Eleusis vase and notice how the spaces between the figures are occupied by rosettes and lozenges and squiggles reminiscent of Miró. It was a long time before the painters, in their move away from the Geometric tradition towards representational painting, reconciled themselves to blank space, and one aesthetic function of labelling figures with names was the occupation of space; sometimes a well-known object, such as a lyre, is labelled unnecessarily, and sometimes a nonsensical sequence of letters fills a gap between figures. The Argive painter of the Cyclops scene evidently felt no compulsion to fill space; he was a century ahead of his time. Understanding of the positive use of emptiness came with the Attic vase-painters of the late 500s and early 400s. It is wonderfully effective when the scene comprises two figures only, one on each side of the vase, starkly isolated against a field of glossy black.

Although there was one genre of vase-painting in which the paint was applied on a whitish ground after the vase had been fired and cooled,

*Above and opposite:* Zeus and Ganymede, on an Attic vase not much earlier than the terracotta statue in colour plate 8. This vase-painter is wholly liberated from the impulse to fill up all the spaces.

nearly all Greek pottery was made in a two-colour scheme, black and brown, the brown ranging from a sandy yellow to the colour which it has become conventional to call 'red'. The colours were fixed by the firing of the pot: after the whole pot had turned red through a high intake of air to the kiln and then black through restriction of the air intake, the basic clay turned back to red when the air supply was opened again, while the areas painted with a solution of finer clay remained black. White and purple could also be achieved by the mixing of appropriate minerals with the clay.

A black-figure or red-figure vase, its colour-contrast fixed by the firing, can be smashed and jumped on and dumped in a bog; thousands of years later, someone digs it up and cleans it and pieces it together, and the colours are as good as new. The same cannot be said of painting on wooden panels, which has almost all perished, or even of frescoes, which have rarely survived without serious fading and damage. One result of this is that pottery is apt to determine our view of the past in a way which

would have surprised the people who made it. Whole tribes or periods are sometimes named after the pottery which characterised them; from the standpoint of the archaeologist or art-historian the 700s BC in the Greek world are, as a whole, the 'Geometric period'. We also treasure the thousands of vases we have from the 500s, 400s and 300s (after which the art died out), not only as satisfying and admirable works of art but also because they illustrate Greek life and the Greeks' perception of their own myths.

And yet, if we had only the literature of the Greeks to guide us, and no surviving fragments of their pottery, we would not have known that they decorated their pottery at all. No vase-painter is ever mentioned by name in Greek literature; such of their names as we know are derived entirely from signed vases. When the Greeks spoke of painters they meant people who painted on a grand scale on the interior walls of temples and public buildings. Our knowledge of that – of *real* painting – has to be derived essentially from descriptions or, on occasion, from much later copies and imitations. Only very recently, thanks to the discovery of the Macedonian royal tombs at Vergina, has it been possible for us to make direct acquaintance with great painting of the late 300s BC. Compared with that, vase-painting was a minor art operating within a very narrow range of artistic conventions.

CHAPTER FIVE

# The Oresteia

## Agamemnon's Homecoming

Not so long ago it was believed that the Greeks invented drama. It was always a rash claim, because any number of human cultures in the remotest past may well have enjoyed performances in which the performer pretended to *be* someone else instead of simply singing or speaking *about* someone else; to recite 'She had so many children she didn't know what to do' is not drama, but to dress up as a woman and cry 'I have so many children I don't know what to do' is. Now we have good evidence that the Egyptians performed some of their religious rituals in dramatic form, long before the Greeks.[50] But it is still true that the Greeks were the first people so far known to us to compose powerful and serious plays about human beings behaving in complicated and unpredictable human ways, plays written in a poetic language to which the occasional echo of ritual and ceremonial formulism is only incidental.

There is a paradox here. Performances of Greek drama were part of a religious festival in honour of a god. Practically all of them presented myths about 'heroes' and 'heroines', of mixed divine and human parentage, worshipped with prayer and sacrifice in shrines and sanctuaries all over the place. In many Greek plays gods and goddesses appear as characters. The explanation of the paradox is not that the Greeks made their art religious (as is sometimes said), but rather that they made their religion artistic. They put drama into a festival because they enjoyed it, and they therefore expected the god to enjoy it and to feel honoured by the artistic embellishment of his festival. Religion did not always have to be solemn or frightening or divorced from the pleasures of the senses. And the divine and half-divine figures of Greek tragedy are not remote and mysterious; modifying a sentence in the paragraph above, we can say that the Greeks composed plays about gods, heroes and human beings all behaving in complicated and unpredictable human ways.

The early history of Greek tragedy is dominated by Aeschylus, seven

of whose plays survive. Of his predecessors very little is known. On one
occasion (458 BC) in the last years of his life he put on a 'trilogy', i.e. a
set of three tragedies, known as the *Oresteia*; individually, they are
*Agamemnon*, *Choephori* ('Libation-bearers') and *Eumenides* ('Kindly
ones', a prudent name for the frightening Furies). Actually, a Greek tragic
poet was normally required to put on a 'tetralogy', a set of four plays
of which the fourth was much more frivolous in type, but we no longer
have the fourth play that went with the *Oresteia*. Aeschylus liked to
take the opportunity to write three tragedies about successive stages of
the same myth, as if they were three acts of one gigantic tragedy, and the
*Oresteia* is a set of that kind. The practice was not compulsory, and
most dramatists did not follow it; nor did Aeschylus always.

*Agamemnon* is about the homecoming of Agamemnon, the commander of the great Greek army which fought the Trojan War and
destroyed Troy. The myth is long-established and widely known; everyone in the audience knows that Agamemnon is going to be murdered by
his wife Klytaimestra ('Clytaemnestra') and her lover, his cousin Aigisthos.
The play begins quietly, with a watchman on the palace roof waiting
for the sight of a beacon in the dark which will tell him that Troy has
fallen. Suddenly he sees it; ten years of weary suspense are over. He goes
off to arouse Klytaimestra; but before he goes he hints to us that all is
not well in Agamemnon's palace, and this murmur of foreboding will
very gradually become louder and more disturbing as the play progresses.

The chorus comes on, not yet knowing of the beacon. They were too
old for military service even when the expedition left, ten years ago, and
their thoughts are sombre. They sing of an omen that was sighted at the
time of the departure, and of the assembling of the great fleet at Aulis,
when

> Down came winds from the north,
> frustration, hunger, storm at anchorage,
> scattering men, ravaging ships and ropes.
> Day after day the wearing wait
> wrinkled the flower of Greece.
> There was a cure
> more crushing than the hateful storm.
> The seer intoned it to the kings,
> speaking, he said, for Artemis.
> And the sons of Atreus
> thumped their sticks on the ground
> and could not check their tears.

If we know something of the myth, we know what they mean: Kalkhas
the seer said that the omen showed the hostility of Artemis to be the
cause of the adverse winds, and he declared that Artemis could be
appeased only by sacrificing Agamemnon's daughter, Iphigeneia, at the

altar. Now the chorus present us with Agamemnon in his terrible
dilemma.

The king, the leader, spoke aloud:
'A hard fate, to disobey the seer;
a hard fate, if I must slay my child,
light of my house,
and at the altar stain a father's hands
with virgin daughter's blood.
Here are no ways that do not lead to ill.

Can I desert,
failing my allies?
Why should they not desire,
with passion above all passion,
a virgin's blood, a sacrifice
to stop this wind?
Well ... may good come of it!'

And when the overmastering yoke was on him,
his spirit veering,
blowing foul, impure, unholy,
then his mind was set on course
to the unthinkable.
For mortal men grow bold
when shame is overturned within their thoughts
by evil madness,
lighting a train of suffering.
And he – yes, he sacrificed his daughter,
to speed a war about a stolen wife
and play the battle-fleet to sea.

She begged, she cried her father's name.
The leaders brushed aside her pleas,
a girl's life;
their verdict was for battle.
Her father spoke the prayer of sacrifice.
She clung upon his robes despairingly.
He told the servants
to lift her like a kid above the altar,
high, facing down,
and clamp a guard upon her lovely lips,
a bit to make her dumb,
to check by force
a cry imperilling his house.

Her yellow skirt was billowing to the ground.
Her eyes, in search of pity,
were piercing, one by one, her slaughterers,
a beauty in a painting

yearning to call their names;
for often had she sung within the palace
when men were gathered at her father's feasts,
in pure voice of a girl unpierced,
honouring the god, asking for future blessings
upon the offering of wine
by the father whom she loved.

What happened then, I did not see,
nor do I tell it.[51]

It is for us to build up the scene in our mind's eye as the song of the chorus presents us with the vivid details, one after another, charged with pathos. The Greek theatre would not have tolerated a simulation on stage of a girl's throat being cut; that Iphigeneia's throat was indeed cut, the last two lines of the passage tell us with sadness and dignity.

But what does the chorus tell us about Agamemnon? They use violent language in condemning his choice: foul, impure, unholy, evil, mad. Yet their description of his dilemma – a scrupulous description, one might say – is at odds with their emotional reaction, and when we look at it through Greek eyes, the discrepancy increases. Agamemnon was told by a distinguished seer what he must do to appease the gods. If he refused, he was violating his oath of alliance (and thereby offending the gods by whom he had sworn the oath) and selfishly frustrating his allies out of regard for his own feelings and his own family. He acknowledges that they are right to expect him to sacrifice his daughter. Other myths, the subject of stirring patriotic tragedies later in the century, told of parents who had nobly sacrificed their daughters at the command of an oracle, to save their country. What about the words which I have translated as 'when the overmastering yoke was on him', literally 'when he went under the yoke-strap of necessity'? Some scholars who have studied the *Agamemnon* are sure that Agamemnon made a free, wicked choice; he sinned, and he *deserved* his subsequent fate. Others are equally sure that he had no choice at all; he committed a horrible act under inescapable compulsion, which *caused* his wife to become an implacable enemy. The fact is that Aeschylus uses a word which sometimes means 'go under (voluntarily)' and sometimes 'be put under (by force)', and his word for 'necessity' is also used of pressures and predicaments from which one *can* escape. That is to say, Aeschylus does not allow the chorus to say whether Agamemnon was free to choose or not; and life is like that. Moreover, he does not allow the chorus to say, either now or in later references to what happened at Aulis, whether or not Artemis demanded the sacrifice of the girl. The great seer *said* she did, and what is a commander to do when his professional seer tells him what the gods want? In several passages of Greek poetry and drama we encounter a commander robustly rejecting a seer's advice, or wryly obeying it, or making a cynical comment on it, and conflict between seer and commander was a fact of life in and after Aeschylus' time. One cannot know for sure in advance, but only when it is too late; that is one of the motifs of the *Oresteia*. The chorus *describes* Agamemnon's dilemma fairly, then *reacts* to the outcome as men do react.

Klytaimestra tells the old men about the beacon, and a messenger arrives, confirming that Troy has fallen. Time passes – a choral song, intervening between scenes of dialogue, has no dimension in dramatic time – and Agamemnon himself arrives. We might expect him to show exuberant affection for the wife he has not seen for ten years, but he speaks instead to the chorus. So does Klytaimestra, at first, turning to Agamemnon only when she has to explain why their son, Orestes, has been sent away. Her description of her years of anxious waiting is extravagant, and her welcome rises to a fulsome climax:

> But now
> my heart is freed from sorrow. I proclaim him
> watchdog of the homestead,
> cable that saves the ship,
> deep-roooted pillar of a lofty hall,
> a father's only child,
> a glimpse of land when sailors' hopes were lost,
> a smile of fortune breaking through the clouds,
> a flowing spring for thirsty travellers.
> When I salute him with these words of praise,
> let none be jealous; many are the ills
> we bore before.
>  And now, my dearest husband,
> step down; but do not put upon the ground
> the feet, my lord, that trampled Troy to death.

At a word from her, slaves come forward and spread on the ground, from Agamemnon's cart to the palace door, swathes of delicate embroidered fabric. It is deep red, like a river of blood, and possibly the patterns on it are white and gold, like fat and guts. But it is not the 'red carpet' familiar to us on ceremonial occasions, for carpets are meant to be walked on, and it becomes clear that Klytaimestra's red cloth will be ruined by heavy feet and dirty, stony ground. Agamemnon is taken aback. His response is censorious.

> Daughter of Leda, guardian of my house,
> your speech has matched my time away from home –
> too long. Due praise
> in fitting terms I should receive from others.
> And for the rest, this womanish pampering,
> this grovelling Eastern flattery, is wrong.
> Do not call down resentment on my path

by spreading robes. Such honour is the gods'.
A mortal man tread upon woven beauty?
How can I without fear? Not as a god
should you revere me, but in human ways.
Men do not say the same of costly cloth
and rags to wipe the feet. God's greatest gift
is to know right from wrong.
No life can be called happy till it's ended.
If I can always do as I have done,
my hope is high.

But Klytaimestra is prepared to argue and determined to win.

KLYTAIMESTRA: Now tell me, as you truly think –
AGAMEMNON:                                              Be sure,
   my answer will be faithful to my thought.
KLYTAIMESTRA: Would you, in fear, have made the gods a vow
   to do this act? (*with a gesture to the red cloth*)
AGAMEMNON:                          Why, yes, if its performance
   were by a seer's prescription.

She is exploiting here a notion which surfaces now and again in Greek
literature: vow to sacrifice whatever it hurts you most to lose, and the
gods will look kindly upon you. Agamemnon's reply is a startling
reminder to us of his decision at Aulis to obey the seer; the chorus
described him, at a point early in the play, as 'not finding fault with any
seer'. Now Klytaimestra uses a second argument.

KLYTAIMESTRA:                                         Priam, now –
   if *he* had conquered, what would *he* have done?
AGAMEMNON: I think, for sure, he would have walked on robes.
KLYTAIMESTRA: Well then, have no regard for *human* spite.
AGAMEMNON: Ah, but the people's murmuring has great power.
KLYTAIMESTRA: He who incurs no spite has earned no fame.

An odd argument. The 'barbarian', 'Eastern', 'Asiatic' character of pomp
and flattery was exactly what Agamemnon objected to, and here is
Klytaimestra suggesting to him that he should model himself on the old
king of Troy. She seems to be trying to touch the nerve that insinuates,
'Come on, be a *man*! Why *shouldn't* you?', playing upon a man's fear
of being outdone in boldness by his adversary (even a dead adversary)
and upon the secret satisfaction of being envied, even when envy implies
malice. Agamemnon has no direct answer, and his new tack lays him open
to cajolery.

AGAMEMNON: (*puzzled*) It's not a woman's part, to show such fight.
KLYTAIMESTRA: In triumph a concession is becoming.
AGAMEMNON: Do you so value victory in this contest?

KLYTAIMESTRA: Do as I ask. If of your own accord
                you grant my wish, you still are in command.

This plea to his magnanimity, casting him in the role of a royal dispenser of happiness, at last topples his resolve.

AGAMEMNON: (*after a moment's reflection*) If this is what you want ...
                (*To a slave*) Come now, undo my boots, those humble slaves
                who guard my feet. And when I tread on tints
                worthy of gods, may no resentful stare
                light on me from afar. I am ashamed
                to squander my inheritance underfoot,
                ruining wealth and fabrics bought with silver.

In saying 'from afar' he is thinking of gods, not men; and he feels (as we are apt to do) that he may mitigate their resentment if, while doing what angers them, he declares openly that he is ashamed of doing it. As he steps down on to the fabric, he gestures towards a silent, veiled figure in the cart.

        Now, this girl, this stranger: take her in
        with kindness; if the conqueror is gentle,
        the gods afar look on him with good will;
        none ever *chose* the yoke of slavery.
        She has come with me as my army's gift,
        the choicest flower of all the spoils of Troy.
        Now since you have subdued me to your bidding,
        I walk a crimson path into my palace.[52]

If we know our Homer, we know that the girl is Kassandra, most beautiful of all Priam's daughters. We also recall an occasion in the *Iliad* on which Agamemnon publicly declared that he preferred a certain captive concubine to his wife Klytaimestra. We are aware that Kassandra has been given to him as a bedmate, not as a handmaiden, and that neither in the classical period nor in the heroic age does a returning husband expect his wife to accept without a tremor the importation of a second woman. We wonder what kind of man Aeschylus' Agamemnon is meant to be. Callous towards his wife, for sure, and his moralising about the gods' approval of kindness towards slaves would impress more if it were not uttered in the interests of his own concubine. But does Aeschylus mean us to believe that Agamemnon already knows, and has known for a long time, that Klytaimestra has a lover? His first speech on his arrival – to the chorus – certainly struck a note of menace. Unfortunately, we do not see or hear so very much of Agamemnon in the play that bears his name, and we shall now hear no more of him except his cry when he is mortally stabbed in his bath indoors.

    Kassandra ignores all invitation and urging to enter the palace, and is left on-stage with the chorus. We soon see why Aeschylus has brought her into the play; for she is a seer, a clairvoyant, to whom visions of past and future present themselves when she is supernaturally possessed. The scene that follows is one of the most original and spectacular in extant Greek tragedy, and it has the effect of building up an insupportable tension as we wait for Agamemnon's death.

The chorus is startled and shocked when the shrinking captive suddenly breaks into movement and voice with wild crying on the name of Apollo, in terms that belong unmistakably to the grief and despair of funerals, not at all appropriate to the homecoming of a victorious king. But they recognise that she is possessed, and when she demands of Apollo, 'Where have you brought me? What *is* this house?', the chorus-leader spells out a careful answer, assuring her that it is Agamemnon's palace.

> KASSANDRA: Ah! No!
>   A house the gods hate,
>   conscience heavy with ills,
>   murder of kindred,
>   a slaughterhouse of men,
>   a floor splashed!
> CHORUS-LEADER: I think this woman from Troy has a keen nose,
>   like a hound. She is tracking murder – asking, whose? – and she
>   will find out.
> KASSANDRA (*staring up at the roof*): Yes!
>   *There* is the proof I trust!
>   There! Children crying slaughter,
>   the roasting of their flesh,
>   eaten by their father!
> CHORUS-LEADER: Yes, we had heard that you are a seer, but we are
>   not seeking people who will tell what the god reveals to them.

Kassandra's vision of children killed and eaten is a glimpse of truth well known to the chorus: Agamemnon's father Atreus killed and cooked the children of his brother Thyestes, and Thyestes cursed Atreus' family. Now Kassandra sees another vision, at first obscurely threatening, then taking on an unpredictable succession of vivid shapes.

> KASSANDRA: Oh! Oh!
>   What is this plot?
>   What is this horror *now*?
>   A monstrous, monstrous plot
>   within this house!
>   A blow to crush the family,
>   an ill beyond all cure.
>   And I see no help, no help.

CHORUS-LEADER: In these prophecies I am lost. What you said before,
   I understood; why, it is the talk of all the city.
KASSANDRA: Woman, woman!
   Is *this* what you will do?
   Wash him bright in the bath,
   your man, mate of your bed,
   and – how can I speak the end?
   So soon it will come.
   A hand reaches out,
   and a hand, stretching.
CHORUS-LEADER: I don't understand yet. Now I'm in confusion.
   These riddles – there is the darkness of oracles in them.
KASSANDRA: Ah! Ah! What's this appearing?
   Is it a net of Death?
   Why, *she*'s the snare!
   His bed was hers,
   his murder's hers.
   Let strife that leaves the house no peace
   cry on the sacrifice.
   Stoning revenge will come.
CHORUS-LEADER: What Fury is this that you command to raise a cry
   over the house?
   There is no cheer in your words for me.
   Over my heart it flows,
   the pallid blood of fear,
   as in a man
   slain by a sword,
   when the sun sets on his life
   and doom is swift.
KASSANDRA: Oh! Look! Look!
   Keep the bull from the cow!
   It's like a robe.
   With a black horn –
   *that*'s how she strikes. He falls,
   the water wraps him round.
   I tell you,
   treacherous death in a bath,
   that is his fate.[53]

Even when Kassandra turns her prediction into plain language and tells the chorus that Agamemnon is going to be killed, they find it hard to grasp. Despite the visions which we have just heard her describe, their imagination is simply closed to the possibility that the warrior-king will be killed by a *woman*.

Yet he is, and Kassandra with him. Then Klytaimestra, by turns exultant, defiant, bitter, argumentative, confronts the chorus, and we are now told explicitly for the first time in the play that she is the lover of

Aigisthos, the youngest child of Thyestes and the only one to escape
when his brothers and sisters were killed and cooked. Aigisthos himself
appears in the last scene, and a chain of cause and effect, built up
throughout the play by increasingly explicit allusion, is completed.
Agamemnon has perished in fulfilment of the curse on the family which
his father's crime wrung from Thyestes.

But Agamemnon's family is not yet extinct. His son Orestes is safe
and out of reach.


### Killing Mother

In the second play of the trilogy, *Choephori* (*Libation-bearers*),
Orestes returns with his friend Pylades, the son of the man to whose
keeping his mother had entrusted him. He puts locks of his hair as
offerings on Agamemnon's tomb.

Klytaimestra has had a vivid and frightening dream, that she was
suckling a snake which drew blood from her breast. Believing, as many
Greeks did, that such a dream might be an intervention by a supernatural
power outside herself, she tries to appease the ghost of Agamemnon by
sending their daughter Elektra to offer libations and prayers at his tomb.
It is not easy for Elektra to be the mouthpiece of her hated mother in
this futile attempt to placate her murdered father; at the prompting of the
slaves with her (the chorus of the play) she prays instead for the return
of Orestes. Then she sees the hair he left on the tomb, hair like hers, and
her heart leaps with hope. At the sight of footprints on the ground like
hers in shape, she realises that Orestes may be there in person. He comes
forward and declares himself, clinching the proof of his identity (they
have not seen each other since childhood) by showing her a garment in
his possession which she herself had woven.

Brother and sister, together with the chorus, invoke the gods of the
underworld and their father's ghost. Whereas in Aeschylus' *Persians* the
ghost of Darius, invoked by the chorus, appears and speaks, in *Choephori*
Agamemnon's ghost remains unseen and silent; his presence has to be felt,
and is. Orestes declares his plan: he and Pylades will pretend to be
travellers from Phokis bringing news of Orestes' death, and so gain
entrance to the palace.

This they do. Klytaimestra welcomes them in, and sends a slave,
Orestes' old nurse, to bring Aigisthos with his bodyguard. The chorus,
hinting to the nurse that things are not what they seem, persuade her to
change that 'with his bodyguard' to 'without a bodyguard'. So Aigisthos
comes alone and walks in to where his killers are waiting for him. We
hear his scream as the sword goes into him, and the play explodes into
a violence and speed contrasting very strongly with the leisurely pace at
which it has hitherto developed.

(*A slave tears in and rushes to the door which represents the door of the women's quarters*)

SLAVE (*shrieking*): Aigisthos! He's dead!
   Open! Quickly! Unbar the women's door!
   We need a fighting man – but not to help,
   help's too late. It's done. No use. Hi! Hi!
   I'm crying to the deaf. They're all asleep.
   I shout, and nothing happens. Where's the queen?
   What's Klytaimestra doing?
   How near her throat is to the butcher's block,
   her head to tumbling at the stroke of Justice!

KLYTAIMESTRA (*striding out of the door*):
   What is it? What's this shouting in the house?

SLAVE: Madam ... the dead have come to kill the living.
   (*He stares at her for a moment, then runs away, deserting a lost cause*)

For a moment Klytaimestra despairs, then her fierce pride revives. She killed her husband, and now she must try to kill her son to save her own life. She is too late.

KLYTAIMESTRA: Ah!
   I read your riddle.
   By treachery we killed; so shall we die.
   Quickly! Bring me an axe to kill a man!
   (*but no one obeys this order*)
   We'll see at last whether we win or lose.
   *This* is our moment of extremity.

(*Enter Orestes and Pylades, swords drawn*)

ORESTES (*pointing to Klytaimestra*): It's *you* I seek.
   (*Gesture back towards palace*) To *him* I've done enough.

KLYTAIMESTRA: Dead? O my brave Aigisthos, are you dead?

ORESTES: You love him? Well ... you'll share his grave,
   and never fail him there.

KLYTAIMESTRA: (*ripping open her dress and cupping her left breast in her hand*): Stop! My son!
   My child! Honour this breast!
   So often, here, before your teeth were grown,
   you dozed and sucked the milk that made you strong.

For all his resolution, Orestes wavers. He turns to Pylades, and Pylades utters the only words – momentous, decisive words – that we hear from him in the whole play:

ORESTES: Pylades, what shall I do? Am I to shrink
   from killing her – my mother?

PYLADES: What then becomes of those prophetic words,
   Apollo's oracle, and our sworn pledge?
   Count all men enemies rather than the gods.

Pylades knows that mankind shrinks from a man who kills his mother. But Orestes has asked the oracle at Delphi what he should do, and Apollo has given him a clear command: kill her.

ORESTES: Yes ... good advice. You are in the right.
   (*to Klytaimestra*) Come! I shall kill you at his side.
   You rated him in life above my father.
   Sleep with him, then, in death. This man you love,
   and hate the husband whom you should have loved.
KLYTAIMESTRA: I fed you, and I would grow old with you.
ORESTES: What! Live with me? You who killed my father?
KLYTAIMESTRA: Fate has her share of blame for what was done.
ORESTES: And is not your death too the work of Fate?
KLYTAIMESTRA: Have you no reverence for a parent's curse?
ORESTES: You – parent – cast me out into misfortune.
KLYTAIMESTRA: Not 'cast'; it was to friends I sent you safe.
ORESTES: Son of a free man, sold disgracefully!
KLYTAIMESTRA: Where is the price that I received for you?
ORESTES: I am ashamed to put that charge in words.

He means: you were able to take Aigisthos as a lover when you had got rid of me. Klytaimestra flares up.

KLYTAIMESTRA: Then say the same about your father's follies!
ORESTES: You stayed at home. He laboured. Do not blame him.
KLYTAIMESTRA: A separation from a man, my child,
   is pain to women.
ORESTES:         Yes, but while they stay
   indoors, his toil sustains them.
KLYTAIMESTRA:         O my child,
   your purpose ... you are going to kill your mother?
ORESTES: Yours is the hand, not mine, that ends your life.
KLYTAIMESTRA: Take care! Beware a mother's angry hounds!
ORESTES: How can I flee my father's, if I fail him?

Klytaimestra has lost. Only despair remains to her, and its pathos will not deter Orestes now.

KLYTAIMESTRA:         The living mourner cries; the tomb is deaf;
   I am the mourner.
ORESTES:         Yes; my father's fate
   has sentenced you to death.
KLYTAIMESTRA:         Alas for me,
   *this* is the snake that nestled at my breast.
   The fear that came in dreams was prophecy.
ORESTES: You killed a husband; now a son kills you.[54]

Those last words in Greek are literally 'You killed (him) whom you ought not, and now undergo what ought not (to be)', and they illustrate one kind of problem which is constantly faced by the translator of Greek drama. There is another problem at the beginning of the piece, which I have simply ducked, for the slave runs in crying, literally, 'Alas, all-alas for master struck! Alas again in third addressing! Aigisthos is no more!' That a man in such circumstances should comment on the number of times he is saying 'Alas!' is alien to English poetry, and the point here, that it was customary to utter a triple farewell to the dead at a funeral, cannot be brought out by translation alone; it needs a footnote. Greek poetry was strongly differentiated in language from prose and speech, and its metrical forms were exceedingly strict. By contrast, the modern audience of a play translated into verse has limited tolerance of the te-tum-te-tum of the English five-foot line, and in deference to them the translator must exploit the resources of stress and pause in order to spike the regularity.

Greek drama, like Elizabethan drama, cannot always resist a temptation to create an image or conceit in a context to which it has no particular appropriateness. Agamemnon, calling for someone to undo his boots, adds, 'those humble slaves which serve my feet'. When Klytaimestra sees the messenger approaching, she calls the dust that his feet kick up 'sister neighbour of mud'. There are times, too, when the dialogue of two characters in deadly confrontation seems to us organised with excessive formality, each character speaking a twelve-syllable line alternately for twenty or more 'turns'. Klytaimestra's last dialogue with Orestes is an example. Her appeals to his pity, her logical argument ('Fate has her share of blame'), her threats (of 'a parent's curse' and 'a mother's angry hounds'), her rebuttals ('Not "cast"' and 'your father's follies'), her renewed pathos ('a separation from a man' and 'you are going to kill your mother?') – all are parried or demolished by Orestes, as if two opposing speeches in a court of law had been reduced to a succession of single-line arguments and counter-arguments and then interleaved.

But when we penetrate the formal, symmetrically patterned wrapping, don't we find that the mixture of pathos, threat, and logic is exactly the mixture that people in real life concoct when they desperately need to win? In rather the same way Orestes earlier in the play, explaining his resolve to avenge his father, does not say simply that the god has commanded it, or simply that his sense of honour will give him no rest, or anything simple. He says that Apollo has commanded his act of vengeance and has threatened horrible punishments if he fails to perform it, *and* that he grieves for his father, *and* that he needs to recover his inheritance, so that he may escape from unworthy poverty and the men of his city, conquerors of Troy, may no longer suffer the shame of obedience to 'two women' (his mother and her cowardly lover). It is true to life that a man trying to rouse himself to the commission of an act both dangerous and abhorrent should fortify reasons of one kind by reasons of another.

Greek tragedy is about deities in whom we do not believe and about heroes and heroines who may never have existed and who, if they did exist, were in any case not 'larger than life'. Yet simultaneously it was, as has been said recently,[55] 'about people and what they do to each other'. These 'people' are not a separate lot from the heroes and deities; the heroes are people and, as we shall see when we come to look at the third play of the trilogy, deities are people too. The characteristic predicaments of tragedy are unusual; few of us, after all, do as Oedipus did, killing men who turn out afterwards to be our fathers and marrying women who turn out to be our mothers; few of us sacrifice our daughters in obedience to an oracle or seer. Does that matter? Desires, fears and hatreds which we hesitate to expose in casual conversation, or even to anyone ever, are deeply lodged within us, and Greek tragedy brings them out into the open. That is why some myths are so tenacious. If we generalise tragic predicaments, we recognise our own experience in tragedy: the obstinate adherence to a choice made in doubt and haste, or the destruction of something which we love (our own lives, among other things) for the sake of good repute and in fear of humiliation.

### Resolution

In *Eumenides*, the third play of the trilogy, there are only two human characters: Orestes, and the priestess at Delphi who speaks the prologue. The rest are deities – Apollo, Athena, and the chorus of Furies – or from the underworld, Klytaimestra's ghost.

The Furies are a group of female beings, filthy, ugly and malevolent, conjured up by the killing of Klytaimestra and now in relentless pursuit of Orestes; they are his 'mother's angry hounds'. He has fled to the sanctuary of Apollo at Delphi. Apollo has purified him, and promises to sustain him to the end; he tells him to go to Athens, to appeal to Athena, and submit to trial. The Furies have fallen asleep around Orestes in the temple, and when he has gone (escorted, under Apollo's instructions, by the god Hermes) the ghost of Klytaimestra appears and awakens the Furies by intervening in their dreams.

> KLYTAIMESTRA: Yes, you can sleep! And what's the use of sleepers?
> So you reject me, and among the dead,
> unceasingly reviled for those I killed,
> I am disgraced, an outcast. And I tell you,
> none bears a greater burden of reproach.
> My fate was cruel, from those that owed me love;
> and yet no god is wrath on my behalf,
> the victim of a hand that killed a mother.

See – in your hearts – these wounds!
For though by day the lot of men is hidden,
a mind asleep has eyes; the light pours in.
O, many an offering of mine you lapped,
libations without wine, a sober charm;
I gave you solemn feasts before the hearth
at dead of night, an hour no god will share.
All this I see now trampled in contempt,
while *he* is gone, escaping like a fawn –
one nimble jump out of your net's embrace.
Now *I* am at stake. Hear what I say,
heed me, goddesses from below the earth.
I, Klytaimestra, call you in a dream!

(*The Furies utter a whining noise in their sleep*)

Yes, whine! But the man is gone in flight,
far off! *His* friends take heed of his entreaty.

(*A louder whine*)

You slumber deep. No pity for my fate!
Orestes has escaped – my son, my killer.

(*A deeper noise from the Furies*)

You groan, you slumber. Will you not spring up?
What is your task, if not to persecute?

(*More groaning from the Furies*)

Labour and sleep in strong conspiracy
have sapped the fury of the fearful snake.

(*The Furies stir in their sleep*)

CHORUS: Get him ... get him ... get him ... Look ... look ...

KLYTAIMESTRA: In dream you chase a beast, with yelping voice,
like hounds whose thirst for blood gives them no peace.
Get up! Act! Toil must not subdue you,
nor sleep dispel your anguish. Stab your heart
with just reproach – a goad that spurs the righteous.
Breathe on your victim's track a gale of blood,
wither him with your breath, your belly's fire;
After him! Wear him down! Renew the chase![56]

The ghost vanishes; the Furies rouse themselves and set off in pursuit.

Arriving at Athens, Orestes casts himself as a suppliant at a statue of
Athena and invokes her aid. The Furies have caught up with him, and
they agree, confident in the justice of their cause, that Athena shall
arbitrate. She convenes a jury of Athenian citizens, and before this jury
the Furies and (on behalf of Orestes) Apollo conduct themselves with
the vehemence of human litigants. The Furies' case rests on the principle
that mother and child are 'of one blood', while husband and wife are
not. Apollo, who insists that he speaks with the authority of Zeus, denies
genetic connection between mother and child; the seed is the father's, and
the mother's womb is only the seed-bed. The Furies threaten the jury

with harm to the land of Attica, Apollo bribes it with the promise of blessings, including the eternal friendship of Argos. Athena declares that if the votes are equal, she will give her casting vote for acquittal, because she, though a virgin goddess, 'favours the male in all things' and is 'wholly on the father's side'; and when the votes prove to be equal, she is as good as her word. Orestes departs with a renewed promise of Argive friendship for Athens.

The rest of the play is not about him, but about Athens. The Furies are at first irreconcilably vengeful, threatening blight and sterility. By patience and courtesy, Athena persuades them to accept an honoured sanctuary for all time at Athens.

People ask, sometimes in portentous voice and with a keen glare in their eyes, 'What is the *Oresteia about*?' They are not content with the answer, 'It's about the killing of Agamemnon by his wife Klytaimestra, the killing of Klytaimestra by their son Orestes, and the acquittal of Orestes at Athens', because they would prefer to be told 'justice', 'mercy', 'the evolution of society', and the like. But even without going to that level of abstraction, there is reason for discontent with the bald statement that the *Oresteia* is about murders in the family of Agamemnon. Let us have another shot.

Four strands in the *Oresteia* can easily be discerned. First, there is the inherited myth of Agamemnon, Klytaimestra, Aigisthos and Orestes, a myth to which reference is made several times in the *Odyssey* and which was the subject of an important long poem by the lyric poet Stesikhoros a hundred years before the *Oresteia*. (We know that in Stesikhoros' story Orestes was pursued by Furies and helped by Apollo, who gave him a magic bow, but we don't know how Stesikhoros resolved the issue.) The second subject is the origin of the sanctuary and cult of the Furies at Athens, where they were worshipped under the titles of *Semnai theai*, 'revered' (or 'awe-inspiring') 'goddesses', and *Eumenides*, 'kindly ones'. A third subject is the origin of the Athenian homicide court which met on the Areopagus; and a fourth, the origin of Athens' friendship with Argos.

The third and fourth subjects are historically interconnected, in so far as during the last few years before the production of the *Oresteia* a strong democratic faction had become dominant at Athens. In consequence, the alliance with Sparta which had lasted since the Persian invasion was abrogated and replaced by an alliance with Sparta's enemy, the democratic city of Argos; for this reason Aeschylus made Agamemnon king of Argos, ignoring the existence of Mycenae, which had recently been obliterated by Argos (Stesikhoros, also for political motives, had substituted Sparta for Mycenae). The Athenian democrats also restricted the powers of the Areopagus to the hearing of prosecutions for wilful homicide, alleging that that was its ancestral function. Neither of these two topics, the Argive alliance and the origin of the Areopagus, had any connection with the origin of the sanctuary of the Furies, nor did any of the three topics have any connection with the myth of Orestes, until Aeschylus chose to put them all together into one story (a reference in Homer to a stay at Athens by Orestes, even though *before* his return to seek revenge, may possibly have implanted the idea). In order to join the foundation of the Areopagus with the Orestes myth, Aeschylus had to reject a pre-existing myth about the origin of the name *Areios pagos*, 'Hill of Ares', to the effect that the gods gathered there to try the god Ares on a charge of murder, and substitute another explanation of the name; and this he does in a speech put into the mouth of Athena.

Aeschylus, in fact, did something in the *Oresteia* which was certainly uncommon in Greek tragedy: he made the myth relevant to the politics of his time, not by his treatment of ingredients which it already contained but by inventing additions to it. In the eyes of many modern readers, this diminishes his stature, as if a myth were necessarily a vehicle for eternal verities and propaganda necessarily a contamination. But there is no reason to suppose that Aeschylus sold his soul to anyone – and no reason to imagine that he found the institutions and tradition of his own city less profoundly exciting than the issues raised by the Orestes myth as he inherited it.

What are those issues? I have certainly heard the *Oresteia* called 'a sermon on mercy', although Zeus, through Apollo, commands Orestes *not* to be merciful to his mother, and Orestes at the end is vindicated. It has been said that the trilogy is about an evolution in the divine world, the maturing of divine justice; or about a social evolution, the replacement of the vendetta by the rule of law and trial by jury. These motifs are hardly made clear. The Furies, after all, did not pursue murderers indiscriminately, but only those who murdered blood-relations. And there is nothing in Aeschylus to say (as people said fifty years later) that Orestes should have prosecuted his mother instead of simply killing her; indeed, according to Aeschylus, Zeus, through Apollo, said the opposite. The jury convened by Athena certainly try (literally) 'first case of shed blood', but if Aeschylus meant by that not the first case to be tried by the Areopagus but the first homicide case in human history to be tried by a court, he has not made it easy for his audience to understand him.

But isn't the trilogy in some sense about divine justice? After all, Thyestes cursed Atreus, and Agamemnon paid the penalty. But this is hardly a moral 'lesson' or a religious 'sermon' needed by Aeschylus' audience, which was disposed (and had always been disposed) to believe that the gods sooner or later punish great crimes. We may perhaps come nearest to answering the question 'What is the *Oresteia* about?' if we say that Aeschylus *exploited*, with an eye to the greatest dramatic effect, an old and well-known story, *and* contemporary issues which gave Athens pride and confidence, *and* moral and religious beliefs widely held among Athenians. When I say 'dramatic effect', I don't mean colourful spectacle, frightening noise and cheap thrills that pass in an hour. What makes drama effective is its power to drag us into the predicaments of the characters, so that their experience becomes a permanent part of ours. It can achieve this effect only by making convincing characters utter illuminating words about the things that matter to them, and the things that matter are more often personal and practical than philosophical.

# CHAPTER SIX

# God, Man and Matter

## Socrates, Friends and Enemies

Among the images of the ancient Greeks which float in our minds today one of the most persistent is that of a nation of philosophers spending all their hours of abundant leisure in the market-place arguing about the nature of absolute beauty and the square on the hypotenuse of a right-angled triangle. 'Socrates' is the one Greek name more likely than any other to be recognised by the man in the street today. 'Plato' would run it a close second; and many people who have very little idea of what Plato actually said take it for granted that he is the very essence of Greek civilisation, the mouthpiece of the Greeks, so that any notions which Plato expressed can be taken without more ado as 'the Greek view of life'.

True, the Greeks invented what modern philosophers would agree in calling 'philosophy'; true, Socrates and Socrates' pupil Plato and Plato's pupil Aristotle have had much more influence on the entire history of philosophy in the western world – one could say, even, on the history of intellectual attitudes – than any other philosophical 'school'; and true again, Plato could fairly be regarded as the most original, powerful and skilful prose-writer that the Greek world produced. But when all that is said, it remains also true that during the lifetimes of Socrates, Plato and Aristotle very few Greeks were philosophers or even seriously interested in philosophy. Greek philosophy is something to which later generations, from the death of Aristotle onwards, chose increasingly to attach importance when they looked back at the classical period. The quality of Plato's writing had much to do with that; and so did the personal character of Socrates as Plato presented him. Christians found much in Plato which was not irreconcilable with Christianity, and some early Christian apologists were inclined to treat Socrates as an 'honorary Christian' who lived a few centuries too early.

Socrates, a native Athenian, born in 470 BC, was contemporary with a number of intellectuals who came from widely different parts of the

Greek world and were made welcome by the upper classes at Athens. Some of them gave lectures and wrote treatises. Socrates wrote nothing, and our only access to his teaching is through other people's portrayal of him. The earliest of all portrayals – the only one, in fact, that falls within his own lifetime – is given by Aristophanes in the comedy *Clouds*. It stands alone in representing him as being almost entirely concerned with things which, according to other people who wrote about him, did *not* concern him: teaching in return for payment, teaching verbal and intellectual tricks to those who wanted to win lawsuits by hook or crook, studying the phenomena of the natural world and the technical details of language and poetry. Aristophanes seems to have attached to his figure of Socrates everything that the man in the street distrusted and ridiculed in the intellectual. Here is a specimen passage from *Clouds*, in which a slow-witted but cunning old farmer, deeply in debt and wanting to foil his creditors, is receiving instruction from Socrates:

STREPSIADES (*puzzled*): But look – Zeus, up on Olympos, don't you count *him* a god?

SOCRATES (*incredulous, scornful*): Zeus? What rubbish! There's no Zeus!

STREPSIADES (*awestruck*): What? Well! (*Recovering countenance a bit*) Who makes the rain? You just tell me that, for a start!

SOCRATES (*gesture towards the chorus of the comedy, who represent Clouds*): They do, of course. I'll explain. The evidence is over-whelming. Have you ever seen rain without clouds? *But*, on *your* theory it ought to rain out of a clear sky, with no clouds in sight.

STREPSIADES (*impressed*): Well, by God, that certainly fits with what you were saying. Do you know, honestly, I always thought it was Zeus pissing through a sieve! (*Cackles, then worried again*) But tell me – who does the thundering? That's what gives me the willies!

SOCRATES: *They* thunder – (*portentously*) in *random motion.*

STREPSIADES: Well, you *do* have some ideas! But how do you mean?

SOCRATES (*adopting lecturing manner*): When they are charged with fluid, and the laws of physics set them in movement, they hang low, laden with rain – through the laws of physics – and then, laden, they collide with each other and split – crash!

STREPSIADES: But who makes all those laws to get them moving? Isn't it Zeus?

SOCRATES: Oooooh no! It is *Atmospheric Rotation.*

STREPSIADES: Well, I never realised Zeus wasn't there any longer, but it was Rotation in charge. (*Suspiciously*) But – you still haven't explained to me about the noise, the thunder.

SOCRATES: Didn't I tell you that when the clouds are filled with water they collide with each other and produce a noise by virtue of their density?

STREPSIADES (*a little pugnaciously*): Well, what's the reason for thinking *that*?

Socrates and Strepsiades in a modern Greek production of Aristophanes' *Clouds*. As commonly in modern productions, Socrates is portrayed as the older of the two, but he was in fact a vigorous 46 when Aristophanes wrote *Clouds*.

SOCRATES (*patiently*): I'll explain with reference to your own experience. Have you ever filled yourself up with stew at a festival and then felt a bit funny in your guts, when a rumbling and bubbling runs all through them?

STREPSIADES: By God I have, and they give me terrible trouble when they're upset, and that bit of stew starts thundering – it's a terrible noise. Quiet-like at first – ppp! ppp! Then it steps it up – pppPP! And when I go and shit, it's *thunder* – ppppPPPP!!! – just like the clouds!

SOCRATES: Well, just think what a fart you can produce from that puny belly of yours; and doesn't it stand to reason that the air above us (*points solemnly*) – infinite – can do a great crash of thunder? That, incidentally, is why the words 'crash' and 'crap' resemble each other.[57]

So much for the comic view of Socrates. It is not friendly; at the end of *Clouds* the farmer Strepsiades, repenting of his dishonest intentions at last, when his son, having received a Socratic education, has coolly beaten him up in the course of a quarrel, sets fire to Socrates' school and drives the unfortunate philosophers off stage with blows and missiles.

A very different view is presented by writers of the next generation who had learned from Socrates when they were young men. There were a number of 'Socratic' writers, but the only two whose works have survived entire were Plato and Xenophon. Plato was himself a philosopher who started from foundations which Socrates had laid. Xenophon was many things – a soldier, a biographer, a moralist – but hardly a philosopher; his concern was to give a portrait of a man whose influence on the young he greatly admired. Both Plato and Xenophon showed Socrates pursuing philosophical questions in dialogue with interested friends, disclaiming special knowledge and eliciting from them contributions towards the solutions of the problems under discussion. Plato often sets out these 'Socratic dialogues' in purely dramatic form, sometimes in near-dramatic form enclosed within a narrative framework, the narrator being either Socrates himself or someone reporting what he had been told about Socrates. One of Plato's most brilliant works is the *Symposium*, in which guests at a dinner-party (including Socrates) take it in turn to make a speech in honour of Eros, the deity who personifies sexual love. Late in the night the party is interrupted by the arrival of Alkibiades, drunk and voluble but marvellously articulate. He insists on making a speech in praise of Socrates instead of one in praise of Eros. By this device Plato contrives to show us that Socrates' life accorded with his teaching, that he was exceptionally brave, self-controlled, resistant to pain and fatigue, wise, just and eloquent. We have to imagine the excerpt which follows as spoken by Alkibiades in the lurching style of a very drunk, very well-educated man choosing his words carefully.

But when we hear *you* speak, Socrates, or when we hear someone else
reporting what you've said, even if the reporter's no good at all, all of
us – man or woman or boy – we're overcome, we're spell-bound. I can
assure you all, if it weren't that you'd think I was completely drunk, I'd
have told you, and I'd have sworn it on oath, what effect Socrates' words
have had on *me*, and what effect they still have now. When I listen to
him, my heart pounds ... it's a sort of frenzy ... possessed! ... and the
tears stream out of me at what he says. And I can see a lot of other
people that he's had just the same effect on. I've heard Perikles, I've heard
plenty more good speakers, and I thought they did pretty well, but they
never had an effect like *this* on me. My soul wasn't turned upside-down
by them, and it didn't suffer from the feeling that I'm dirt. But that's
the feeling I get from *him*. Socrates, you're not going to say that isn't
true! And I know very well, at this very moment, if I were prepared to
lend him my ears, I couldn't hold out; the same thing would happen all
over again. He makes me admit that when there's so much I need, I
don't look after *myself* – it's the *country's* business I'm doing. So ... I
just stop up my ears and I run away, as if I were escaping from the
Sirens ... because if I didn't, I'd just sit – beside *him* – until I was an
old man.[58]

Not only does Alkibiades' speech demonstrate, by vivid stories,
Socrates' possession of the virtues which were admired by the Athenians
and by every sensible nation since then; the portrayal of Socrates in
every other Platonic work brings out his courtesy and patience in dealing
with young and old, rich and poor, his self-deprecating humour, his good
will towards those who respond to his questioning by anger or rudeness.
He does not seem to preach from a position of superior insight or
special knowledge, but claims to be 'wise' only in 'recognising his own
ignorance'. In this setting, a glimpse of his fundamental seriousness can
be dazzling; for example, in the *Gorgias*:

Now, please! You're trying to prove me wrong in an *oratorical* way,
like the people in the law courts who think they're proving a point. In
the courts one side gives the impression of proving the other side wrong
when it produces a lot of distinguished witnesses in favour of its case and
the man on the other side produces only one or none at all. But this sort
of proof is of no value at all so far as concerns the truth, because it can
sometimes happen that someone is condemned on false evidence given
by a lot of witnesses who are thought to matter. And so now, on the
subject you're talking about, practically all Athenians, and others too,
will agree with you, if you want to produce them as witnesses in support of your contention that what I say isn't true ... There is only one of
me; but *I* don't agree with you. You don't offer any convincing reason
why I should; you just produce a lot of false witnesses and try to dis-
possess me of my estate, the truth. But if I can't produce you yourself –
you, one man – as a witness on my side, agreeing with the case I'm

making, I don't consider that anything worthwhile has been accomplished in our discussion. And I don't believe you would think so either, unless I – just one man, by myself – bear witness on your side, and never mind about everybody else.[59]

At the age of seventy Socrates was put on trial on a charge of 'injuring the city by not acknowledging the gods which the city acknowledges but introducing novel supernatural powers, and by corrupting the young'. He was condemned by a majority vote and executed. Plato afterwards composed a speech (the *Apology of Socrates*), purporting to be what Socrates said in his own defence; what relation it bears to what he actually said, we do not know. At one point Plato makes Socrates say:

> You might say to me: 'Now, Socrates, won't it be possible for you, if we allow you to leave Athens and live, to say nothing and keep yourself to yourself?' But this is the hardest thing of all to make some of you see. If I say that it would mean disobedience to a divine command, and for that reason it's impossible for me to keep myself to myself, you won't believe me; you'll think I'm pretending. If I say that the greatest good for any human being is in fact to talk and argue every day about goodness and the other subjects about which you hear me talking and questioning myself and others, and that a life which is not questioned is no life for a man to live, you'll be even less inclined to believe me, if I say that. But that's how it is, in my opinion; but to make you see it is not easy.[60]

That a virtuous citizen, living in a democracy which prided itself on freedom of speech, a component of a civilisation which welcomed experiment and novelty, should be martyred for his persistence in raising questions in moral philosophy is a paradox. Part of the explanation lies in the fact that toleration wilts under stress. The Athenians had suffered plague, disastrous defeat, starvation and civil war. They wondered what they had done wrong, and many of them felt they had offended the gods by being permissive. The other part of the explanation is indicated by an observation made in passing by a political speaker half a century later:

> Men of Athens, you executed Socrates the sophist because he was shown to have taught Kritias, one of the thirty men who overthrew the democracy.[61]

At the time of Socrates' trial men execrated the memory of Kritias and the 'Thirty Tyrants', whose bloodthirsty rule precipitated the civil war, and that of Alkibiades, whose treason (part real, part imaginary) they blamed for their defeat in the war against the Peloponnesians. Kritias and Alkibiades had undeniably been very close to Socrates. He could not be tried for that, for an oath of amnesty at the end of the civil war made such a charge illegal; but he could be tried on other charges and condemned by jurors who knew in their own hearts why they were condemning him. Xenophon in his memoirs of Socrates is at pains to argue that Kritias and Alkibiades were good enough men so long as they associated with Socrates but went wrong when they ceased to listen to him. And the words put into Alkibiades' mouth by Plato in the passage of the *Symposium* quoted above, 'I just stop up my ears and run away', serve the same apologetic purpose.

### A Geometry Lesson

Plato's *Meno* launches us directly and abruptly into a problem which greatly preoccupied him, a problem which the ancients unhesitatingly treated as philosophical, though nowadays we might classify it differently:

> MENO: Can you tell me, Socrates, is goodness teachable? Or not teachable, but acquired by practice? Or neither acquired nor learned, but something which people have by nature or in some other way?[62]

The word which I have translated 'goodness', *aretē*, is a word about which classical scholars are inclined to make too much of a mystery. It is simply the abstract noun corresponding to an adjective translatable as 'good'. We and the Greeks do not always agree about what constitutes human goodness, but that is a different question, which arises to some degree between any two cultures and is apt to arise also between any two individuals; there is no reason whatever to keep *aretē* in Greek, as if it were untranslatable or indefinable.

The course which the argument takes leads to consideration of the nature of teaching and learning. Socrates asks Meno to call one of his slaves across. With his stick he draws a square in the dust, and the dialogue goes like this (the diagrams and stage-directions are mine, not Plato's):

> SOCRATES: Now tell me, boy, you know that a square is a figure like this?

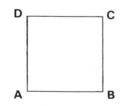

[The word I translate 'square' means simply 'four-cornered', but everything which follows applies to squares alone.]

> SLAVE: Yes, I do.

SOCRATES: So a square's a figure that has all these sides equal, four of them?

SLAVE: Certainly.

SOCRATES: And it has these lines across the middle equal too, hasn't it?

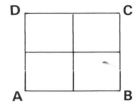

SLAVE: Yes.

SOCRATES: You could have a figure of that kind bigger than this one, or small than this one, couldn't you?

SLAVE: Certainly.

SOCRATES: Well, now: if this side (*he points to AB*) were two feet long, and this one (*he points to BC*) two feet long, how many feet would the whole figure be?

He means, 'How many *square* feet would the figure be?' The slave doesn't answer, and Socrates goes on:

Look at it like this: if it were two feet this way (*pointing to AB*) and only one foot that way (*pointing to BC*), the area would have to be one times two feet, wouldn't it?

SLAVE: Yes.

SOCRATES: But since it's two feet long that way (*pointing to BC*), it's got to become twice two?

SLAVE: Yes, it has.

SOCRATES: So it's twice two feet? [*i.e. square feet*]

SLAVE: Yes.

SOCRATES: Well, how many feet are twice two? Do the sum and tell me.

SLAVE: Four, Socrates.

SOCRATES: Now, could one make another figure, twice as big as this one, but of the same kind, with all its sides equal, like this one?

SLAVE: Yes.

SOCRATES: So how many feet [*i.e. square feet*] will that one be?

SLAVE: Eight.

SOCRATES: Now, let's see: try and tell me how long each side of that second figure will be. The side of *this* one (*pointing at ABCD*) is two feet; and what will the side of the one twice as big be?

SLAVE: Why, obviously, it'll be twice as long, Socrates.

SOCRATES (*turning to Meno*): You see, Meno, how I'm not 'teaching' him anything; I'm *asking* him all the time. Now he thinks he knows the length of the side on which a square of eight feet will be constructed. Isn't that so?

MENO: Yes, indeed.

SOCRATES: Well, *does* he know?

MENO: No, he doesn't.

SOCRATES: But he *thinks* it's on a side double the length?

MENO: Yes.

SOCRATES: Now watch him recollecting, step by step – the right way to recollect.

'Recollection' here picks up the point of all this, which we shall see developed later. Socrates teases out of the slave recognition of the fact that if we double the size of the side of a square we end up with a square not twice its area, but four times its area. The slave then flounders, and suggests we should try a side one and a half times as long. Persuaded that this would produce a square of nine square feet, he volunteers no more suggestions. Socrates makes a fresh start, redrawing the square ABCD.

SOCRATES: Now, tell me: this is our figure, isn't it?

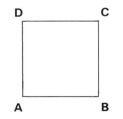

SLAVE: Yes, I've got it.

SOCRATES: Now we can add on another square, the same size? (*Draws in BEFC*)

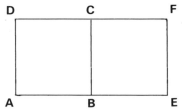

SLAVE: Yes.

SOCRATES: And a third one, here, equal to each of the other two? (*Draws in CFGH*).

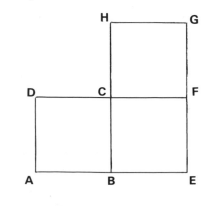

SLAVE: Yes.

SOCRATES: And then we can fill in the one in the corner here. (*Draws in HI and ID*).

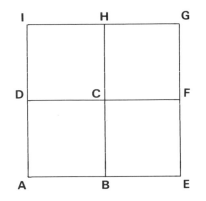

SLAVE: Yes, certainly.

SOCRATES: Then these must be four figures of the same size?

SLAVE: Yes.

SOCRATES: Well, now: this *whole* figure (*points to AEGI*) – how many times as big as *this* one is it? (*Points to ABCD*)

SLAVE: Four times as big.

SOCRATES: But we needed to get one *twice* as big. You remember?

SLAVE: Yes, that's right.

SOCRATES: Well, now, *this* line (*draws in BD, BF, FH, HD*) from corner to corner cuts each of these figures in half? (*Points in turn to ABCD, BEFC, CFGH, DCHI*)

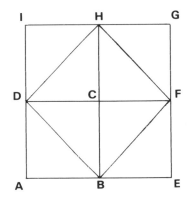

SLAVE: Yes.

SOCRATES: So we've got here four lines of equal length, enclosing this figure? (*Points to BFHD*).

SLAVE: Yes, we have.

SOCRATES: Now, how big is the figure? [*i.e. BFHD*]

SLAVE: Don't know.

SOCRATES: Well, there are *four* squares here, aren't there? (*Points in turn to ABCD, BEFC, CFGH, DCHI*). And each line (*points in turn to BF,, FH, DB*) has cut off half of each square, inside?

SLAVE: Yes.

SOCRATES: And how many figures of that size (*points to the triangle BCD*) are there in this figure (*i.e. BFHD*)?

SLAVE: Four.

SOCRATES: And how many in *this* figure? (*Points to ABCD*).

SLAVE: Two!

SOCRATES: And what's four in relation to two?

SLAVE: It's twice as much.

SOCRATES: And how many feet [*i.e. square feet*] are there in this figure? (*Points to BFHD*)

SLAVE: Eight.

SOCRATES: And what's the line it's on?

SLAVE: This one. (*Points to BD*)

SOCRATES: The one that stretches from corner to corner of that square? (*Points to the square ABCD*)

SLAVE: Yes.

SOCRATES: That's what the professionals call a 'diagonal'. So, if 'diagonal' is its name, what you're saying is that if you start with a square and want to make one twice the size, you make it on the diagonal?

SLAVE: Yes, that's just it, Socrates!

Now Socrates dismisses the slave and turns to Meno in order to draw from this simple lesson in geometry some inferences relevant to the question with which the dialogue started, 'Is goodness teachable?'

SOCRATES: Well, Meno, what do you think? Did he answer with any single opinion that wasn't his own?

MENO: No, it was all his own.

SOCRATES: All the same, he didn't *know*; we agreed that a moment ago.

MENO: That's true.

SOCRATES: But these opinions were *in* him, weren't they?

MENO: Yes.

SOCRATES: So, when a man doesn't *know*, there *are* true opinions *in* him about the things he doesn't *know* about?

MENO: It looks like it.

SOCRATES: At the moment, these opinions have begun to be stirred up in him in a hazy sort of way; but if someone's prepared to ask him these same questions many times and in many ways, you realise that in the end he'll have as precise a knowledge as anyone.

MENO: It seems so.

SOCRATES: And he'll have that knowledge without anyone having taught him, only *asking* him; he'll have recovered the knowledge himself, out of himself.

MENO: Yes.

SOCRATES: And recovering knowledge inside oneself – that's *recollecting*, isn't it?

MENO: Certainly.

SOCRATES: The knowledge he has now – either he was given it at some time, or he had it all the time?

MENO: Yes.

SOCRATES: So, if he had it all the time, he was knowledgeable all the time, but if he was given it on some occasion, he can't have been given it in his present life. Or has anyone taught this slave of yours geometry? He'll do just the same as he did with any part of geometry and any other subject. Has anyone taught him them all? *You* ought to know, considering that he's been born and brought up in your house.

MENO: I know very well that no one's ever taught him.

SOCRATES: And *has* he got these opinions, or not?

MENO: It looks as if he *must* have.

SOCRATES: But if he doesn't have them through being given them in his present life, isn't it clear at once that he had them and understood them at some other time?

MENO: It looks like it.

SOCRATES: And that'll be the time when he wasn't a living human being?

MENO: Yes.

SOCRATES: And if there are going to be true opinions in him both during the time that he's a human being and the time that he isn't, and these opinions are woken up by questioning and turn into knowledge, we shall have to say – shan't we? – that his soul has been in possession of understanding all the time. After all, it's obvious that at *any* time he either *is* a human or he *isn't*.

MENO: That seems to be so.

SOCRATES: Then, if the truth of reality is always in our souls, the soul must be immortal, so that whatever you don't actually know now – I mean by that, whatever you don't actually recollect – you've every reason to try and look into it and recollect it.

MENO: Somehow I think you're right.

SOCRATES: So do I, Meno! Mind you, there are plenty of things I couldn't swear to in defence of my argument; but if we make it our duty to look into what we don't know about, we'd be better, and better *men*, and more *use* than we would be if we thought it wasn't possible to find the answer to what we don't know, or not worth trying – *that*'s something I'll fight for to the end, just as long as I can, in word and action.

MENO: I think you're right about that too, Socrates.

SOCRATES: Well, then ... since we're agreed on the need to look into what we don't know, will you help me in looking into the question, 'What is goodness?'[63]

It is not hard to fault the technique of the dialogue with the slave. Whereas Socrates makes rather heavy weather of twice two, he expects the slave to take twice four in his stride and to remember that the area of ABCD is four square feet. Some of the questions are not genuine questions at all, but clearly convey to the slave that the transversals of a square are equal, that the area of a rectangle is obtained by multiplying the two sides and that a diagonal cuts a square into two equal parts. However, perfect pedagogy might make duller reading, and we must not carp. If it is possible, as Socrates says, to elicit from an uneducated slave the whole of geometry by prodding him into 'recollection', an interesting social conclusion follows: that anyone, in time, can learn anything. This is a surprising 'democratisation' of philosophy by Plato, who was profoundly out of sympathy with the Athenian democracy and committed himself, when he formulated his ideal state in the *Republic*, to a rigid class system. But Plato is full of surprises, and it is wholly mistaken to try to identify his political alignment in terms of any actual political forces of his day. He was equally disillusioned with his native democracy and with the malevolent aristocratic government of the Thirty Tyrants. He spent much time in Syracuse in an unsuccessful attempt to turn the son of the tyrant Dionysios I into a 'philosopher-king'. His ideal state, governed by a ruling class trained in philosophy but denied the enjoyment of private wealth, luxury imports and ostentatious competition between families, contained little to attract the rich. He laid the foundations of the democratisation of philosophy (and of much else), *if* it is true that the 'Socratic method' which he portrayed was peculiar to Socrates and alien to notable teachers contemporary with Socrates. *If* Plato's representation of those teachers in such dialogues as *Protagoras* and *Gorgias* is honest, then the Socratic method *was* something new. But these 'ifs' are very important.

### Faith and Reason

The geometry lesson could have given rise to interesting enquiries into what exactly is going on inside us when we discover something by reasoning and can say, 'I didn't know before, but now I know'. But readers of the passage quoted were, I hope, astonished by Meno's ready acquiescence in Socrates' assertion that the slave's soul *must* have known geometrical propositions before it was united with the slave's body, as if that were the only alternative, or even a plausible alternative, to his having been taught them during his lifetime. We look back at that portion of the *Meno* which precedes the geometry lesson, in the hope of finding some explanation of this nonsense in the form of agreement between Meno and Socrates on a rational argument for the pre-existence of the soul. We are disappointed. They spent some time in testing and rejecting definitions of goodness, a process which led Meno to say, 'If you don't know what it is, how will you recognise it when you find it?'

Socrates in reply invoked the authority of religious experts and the poet Pindar in favour of the belief that the soul is immortal and reincarnated in a succession of bodies. He inferred from this that the soul once knew everything and, if it goes about things the right way, can recover the memory of what it knew. Meno assented, and asked to be told more about 'recollection'.

It commonly happens in Plato's Socratic dialogues that the people who argue with Socrates furnish the base from which Socrates' own line of argument can develop; but as it progresses, their contribution diminishes in significance, so that the dialogue framework becomes a thin disguise for continuous exposition, utilising a great variety of ways of saying 'Yes' and 'Why?'. What is more important, they are apt to agree tamely at the most crucial steps in that exposition, where we expect them to deliver a counter-stroke. Alternatively, a participant in the argument who sticks to his guns may be represented by Plato as obtuse, shallow, boorish or irritable. In a famous passage of the *Republic*, Socrates, answering a young friend's guess at the conclusion towards which he seems to be working, says, 'Well, perhaps; and perhaps even more than that. I don't know yet. Whichever way the argument carries us, like a wind, that way we must go.' Fine words, but not honest words. Plato's Socrates appears on close scrutiny someone quite different from the inquisitive, open-minded Socrates of modern popular tradition. Obsessed with the metaphysics of good and evil, he is wholly devoid of the genuine curiosity which makes a scientist or a historian. So far from being open-minded, he never takes *seriously* – for passion and perplexity are not the same as intellectual respect – any argument which threatens the convictions with which he begins; his concern from first to last is to persuade us of the truth of those convictions. One of his older contemporaries, Protagoras, taught pupils to 'praise and blame the same thing'. This was suspect on moral grounds, as 'making wrong look right', but it was also morally valuable; we should all be wiser people if, whenever we reacted against something, we set ourselves the task of constructing the strongest case we could *for* it, to see how firm that case might be.

Socrates embodied a rebellion against a new and disturbing trend in the philosophy of his time. Xenophanes, long before, had questioned the Greeks' traditional universal notions of the form and attributes of the gods. Xenophanes himself offered instead a more remote and majestic God; but others carried the break with tradition and convention a stage further, questioning the very existence of gods. Protagoras, for example, made the classic statement of the agnostic position:

> On the subject of gods, I am not in a position to know whether they exist or not, or what they look like. Too many things prevent one from knowing: lack of evidence and the brevity of human life.[64]

And Kritias made an impious character in a play suggest, in a long speech which merits consideration independently of its dramatic purpose, that religion had been invented to prop up a social morality which law was unable by itself to sustain:

> When laws restrained mankind from open violence, but men did hidden wrong, then I think some ingenious man propounded the notion that there were gods to fear, so that evildoers might be afraid even if their actions and words and thoughts were hidden.[65]

Disbelief in gods who punish wrong-doing, coupled with the exciting and liberating realisation that much of what we unthinkingly assume to be part of the order of nature is in fact the social convention of our particular time and place, sometimes generated a curious inverted morality, the idea that we 'ought' to be self-seeking and admire those who get away with it.

Socrates seems to have begun with a set of axioms. The first was this: granted that the things and people we encounter in life all change and perish, *there must be something* eternal and unchanging. Well, in a sense there is: a particular beautiful object has a short life, but what about Beauty? We might hesitate to say that Beauty 'existed' before there were living things to find things beautiful, or that it will still exist at some future date when all living creatures have perished; but Socrates did not hesitate. Again, granted that we constantly have to correct and discard items in our 'knowledge' of the world of things and people, in the light of fresh evidence and the discovery of mistakes, Socrates assumed that *there must be some knowledge* which is absolutely secure and beyond correction. Again, in a sense, there is: our knowledge of the relation between the volume of a sphere and its radius is unaffected by the destruction of any particular sphere or a change in the colour of the ink in which the calculations are written. Equally, we can define 'beauty' in such a way that nothing can ever falsify any conclusions we draw from the definition. But Socrates was not content to think that we made such conclusions certain by our own choice of definitions and axioms; he insisted that there could be only one right definition, which represented a discovery of something which *really existed*. Socrates' third axiom, of the utmost importance for the understanding of the way he thinks, becomes apparent in a passage of the *Phaedo*, where he is speaking of an early stage of his own intellectual history:

> I once heard someone reading from a book which he said was by Anaxagoras, explaining how it is Intelligence which orders all things and is the reason for them. That reason pleased me, and I thought it was somehow right that Intelligence should be the reason for everything. . . . I was glad to think that I had found someone of my own way of thinking – Anaxagoras, that is – to teach me about existing things and tell me the

reason for them. I thought he would tell me first whether the earth is flat or round and then, when he had told me that, expound the reason and necessity for it in terms of what is *better*, explaining why it is *better* that the earth should be what it is.[66]

Anaxagoras disappointed Socrates, for he did not explain why nature is best as it is; and Socrates' demand was unreasonable, for it is not at all clear why anyone should expect nature to be either good or bad, and Plato never gets anywhere near to making it clear.

The passages in which Socrates' vision of the world is most powerfully articulated are passages in which Plato shows him preaching, if not to the converted, at least to the receptive and fervently convertible. Socrates becomes at times more like a contestant cheered on by his fans than a philosopher under dissection in a seminar – as, for example, in this key passage from the *Republic*, which I have taken the liberty of turning from the narrative form of the original into dramatic form:

SOCRATES: You know how, when you turn your eyes not on to things whose colours show up in daylight but on to things under the light of the moon or the stars, your eyes are dim, and they seem almost the eyes of blind men, as if there were no clear vision in them.

GLAUKON: Yes, indeed.

SOCRATES: But when they look at things the sun is shining on, they see quite clearly, and there's obviously vision in those same eyes.

GLAUKON: Of course.

SOCRATES: I'd like you to think of the soul in the same way. When it focuses on something which truth and reality shine on, it perceives it and acquires knowledge of it, and it seems to have understanding, but when it turns to what is half in darkness – I mean the mortal world of things that have a beginning and an end – it only has *opinions*, and it's in a haze, and keeps shifting its opinions this way and that, and it doesn't seem to *understand*.

GLAUKON: No, it doesn't.

SOCRATES: Well, now: what invests the known things with truth and gives the man who knows the power to know is actually the Idea of Good. It's what *causes* knowledge and truth. You can think of it as being an object of knowledge. But although both knowledge and truth are beautiful, you'll be right if you regard the Idea of Good as distinct from them and even more beautiful than they are. We said, when we were talking earlier today, that it's correct to think of light and vision as being *like* the sun. In the same way it's correct to think of both knowledge and truth as being like Good, but incorrect to regard either of them as Good; the status of Good is a great deal higher.

GLAUKON: It's an overwhelming degree of beauty you're talking about, if it produces knowledge and truth but surpasses them in beauty. I take it *(slyly)* you're not identifying it with *pleasure*?

SOCRATES: Ough! *(Mock-angry, realising that Glaukon was joking)* Now look at the analogy a bit further – *this* way –

GLAUKON: How?

SOCRATES: I'm sure you'll agree that the sun doesn't only create, in the things we see, the capacity of being seen; it also causes them to come into being, and grow, and it nourishes them, but it isn't itself the same as 'coming into being'.

GLAUKON: Yes, of course.

SOCRATES: Well, in things that are *known*, it isn't just that their being known is created by Good; they *exist*, they are *real*, because of Good, but Good is not the same as reality – it's far beyond reality, more important, more powerful.

GLAUKON: My God! That's going a very, very long way!

SOCRATES (*excusing himself for exciting Glaukon so*): Well, it's your fault. You insist on my telling you what I think about it.

GLAUKON: Yes – and don't stop! Or at any rate go on about the analogy with the sun, if there's any aspect of it you haven't said anything about.

SOCRATES: Why, I've got any amount more to say!

GLAUKON: Do go on, then! Don't leave anything out!

SOCRATES (*wryly*): I think I shall leave out rather a lot. All the same, I'll do the best I can in the circumstances – and I shan't give up.[67]

There is nothing portentous in the presentation of Socrates' doctrine. Its essence here is one of the powerful and essentially simple analogies in which the *Republic* is rich, namely:

| | |
|---|---|
| Sun as cause of coming into being of perishable things. | Good as cause of existence of eternal realities. |
| Sun makes possible opinion founded on vision. | Good makes possible knowledge founded on reason. |

The exposition is charged with modesty and humour; our sympathy is enlisted, and we are drawn into a lively scene. Socrates said to Meno, a propos of the 'recollection' theory, 'There are plenty of things I couldn't swear to in defence of my argument', and in that way disarmed hostile criticism of the peculiar assumption he had made a minute earlier. So on other occasions, too, just when we are being carried away by his eloquent conviction, or resisting it madly, according to our own assumptions and temperaments, he reins back, saying, 'That is the account given, and personally I believe it', or 'Of course, no one could swear that that is true, but I am convinced that if we believe it we shall meet death with courage'. Plato does in the end reveal the extent to which Socratic philosophy is built on faith. If he calculated (and I doubt whether Plato ever wrote a word without calculation) that he would be most likely to convert us by displaying the operation of faith in the life of an extraordinary and attractive man, he did not go far wrong.

Now, Plato was only one of the people who learned from Socrates. There were others who did not agree with Plato or with one another. So, too, the people who learned from Plato – Aristotle is the most famous of them – rejected one or other of the distinctive features of his philosophy and went on to develop their own. We have a great quantity of Aristotle's work, and can study his system in detail.

In the centuries after Aristotle very many of those who accepted classification under particular philosophical labels regarded themselves not as 'Platonists' or 'Aristotelians' but as 'Stoics' or 'Epicureans'. In modern usage 'stoical' is a term applied to fortitude or resignation in pain and suffering, and an 'epicure' is someone who attaches the highest importance to good food and drink. This use of 'stoical' embodies a grain of truth about the Stoics, but Epicurus and his followers had a poor opinion of epicures. The modern terms give no inkling of the fact that Stoic philosophy had much to say about logic and Epicureanism about atoms. The fundamental difference between Stoics and Epicureans lay in their irreconcilable views of the relation between man and his total experience of his environment. The Stoic saw the design and operation of the universe and the unfolding of destiny in historical events as something to be revered as the manifestation of a good and wise purpose, so that human virtue and vice lay in the individual's conformity or conflict with the grand design. The Epicurean, by contrast, saw the universe as the product of chance, a complex of things neither good nor bad in themselves, and praised or blamed the individual human according to his way of coping with circumstances. The keyword of the Stoic teaching was 'duty', that of the Epicurean 'pleasure'; but, so far from advocating luxury and self-indulgence, Epicurus emphasised that the surest way to attain the pleasure which lies in the satisfaction of our desires is to have few and simple desires and to work ourselves free from the irrational fears which stand between us and serenity. Both philosophies could be viewed, in accordance with a long-standing tradition from which Greek philosophy never wholly dissociated itself, as recipes for fortification against suffering. We should, I think, regard the great difference between them as lying not in the details of their many scientific theories – none of which, after all, was demonstrable – but in the religious implications of their approach to such theories. Stoics readily talked the language of religion, though their Zeus was not at all like the lecherous divine ruler of the poets. For Epicurus, removal of the fear of divine punishment was crucial. Out of respect for ordinary human sentiment and practice, he accepted the idea that there are gods, but denied that they care in the least what we do. His gods are simply a different species, of no more relevance to humanity than golden wombats.

We can see plainly enough that Socrates was the great-grandfather of Stoicism. But Epicurus did not devise his philosophy from scratch as a reaction against the Stoics or the Platonic tradition. He too had intellectual ancestors in the classical period: Demokritos, in Socrates' time, and beyond Demokritos a certain Leukippos. Leukippos and Demokritos were the first people to speculate about the atomic structure of matter, to treat chance as the operative force in the evolution of the universe, and to try to explain thought and feeling exhaustively in physical terms. Thus they were 'materialists' in the philosophical and scientific sense of the word —not, of course, 'materialistic' in the sense of preferring a new refrigerator to a silent contemplation of the sunset. We know hardly anything about Leukippos, and the work of Demokritos survives only in quotations from it by later writers. These quotations afford a glimpse of man about whose views on right and wrong most of us would like to know a lot more. For example:

> For all men good and truth are the same, but pleasure is different for different men.
>
> Do not fear the reproach of others more than you fear your own ...
> Fear your own most of all, and let that law be established within you.
>
> It is repentance for what has been shamefully done that sets life right.
>
> He who does wrong is more unfortunate than he who is wrong.
>
> It is right, since we are human, that we should not laugh at human misfortunes but lament them.[68]

We do not know the context of any of these utterances; and if we did, it *might* disappoint us intellectually.

There was a story that Plato wanted to burn the written work of Demokritos, to prevent it from corrupting others. Whether true or false, the story provokes us to ask, 'Would Demokritos ever have wanted to burn the works of Plato?', and it brings out the intensity of the opposition between the two Greek ways of looking at the world. The Socratic-Platonic-Aristotelian-Stoic tradition is in many ways congenial to Christianity, and different elements of it have at different times been absorbed into Christian thought. The alternative tradition, the materialism of Leukippos, Demokritos and Epicurus, is regarded by Marxists as the really important and lasting contribution of Greek civilisation to human thought. The first thing ever published by Karl Marx was on Demokritos.

Christianity would have managed all right without Socrates, and Marxist revolutions would have managed without Demokritos. Greek philosophy is not historically important in the sense that without it the most significant developments in the history of the Western world would not have occurred, but in the sense that a great many people for the last two thousand years have found it interesting and inspiring. As for what is important *to us*, we are free to exercise a certain choice, to decide what we will treat as important.

*Providence and History*

Earlier in this book we heard Egyptian and Mesopotamian kings proclaiming their achievements in boastful narrative inscriptions, glorying in the good will of their gods and the crushing of their contemptible and repulsive enemies. This was not in fact the only kind of historical narrative which the ancient oriental civilisations produced, for we now have many specimens of Babylonian 'chronicles' – spare and concise narratives, ordered in temporal sequence, full of exact quantifications, derived, like the royal inscriptions, from archival material but in general not invested with the extravagant boasting, vilification and religiosity which the kings thought appropriate in telling their subjects about themselves.

There were Greek historical writers in the 500s BC whose work (known to us only from citations) must have had some formal resemblance to the Babylonian chronicles. But the first Greek historian whose work we can read entire – Herodotos, 'Father of History', who was born in the early 400s and died soon after 430 BC – was no chronicler. Getting the events he describes into the right order and assessing the intervals of time between them is often exasperatingly difficult, and there is a good reason for that: for the period he tackled – the conflict between Greece and Asia, from the rise of the kingdom of Lydia down to the Persian invasion of Greece – virtually no archival documentation at all was available to him. By contrast with the Babylonian chroniclers, he was a stylist of exceptionally sensitive judgement, with a very keen eye and ear for drama and pathos, and his entire history, full of anecdotes and digressions and lively dialogue, is wonderfully readable from start to finish. So, it must be said, are the narrative books of the Old Testament, in which the precision of the Babylonian chronicles is often combined with direct speech of a quality and abundance which deprive Greek historical literature of one 'first' (it can, as we shall see, lay claim to some others). The ancestry of the literary technique of Samuel or Kings lies partly in the art of the story-teller, and partly, perhaps, in the abundant dialogue of Mesopotamian epic poetry. The ancestry of Herodotos' technique is to be sought in Homer, whose stories of Troy and of the wanderings of Odysseus are full of speeches and dialogue.

Any given generation in ancient times, it seems, had a tendency to believe that its ancestors were braver, wiser and more virtuous than itself. Homer thought this of the heroes who fought at Troy; when Hektor lifts a great stone to smash the gates of the wall around the Greek ships, Homer comments:

Two men, the best in the land, could not easily heave it up from the ground on to a wagon, such as men are now; but Hektor brandished it easily by himself.⁶⁹

Hesiod, similarly, regards his own time as the worst that has come to pass since man began with the 'golden race' who 'lived like gods', the 'silver race' who were witless creatures, of whom Zeus tired, and the 'brazen race', fierce and pitiless fighters.

> And they [the brazen race] were destroyed by their own hands and went into the dank house of cold Hades, leaving no name behind them. Terrible though they were, black Death took them, and they left the bright light of the sun.
>
> But when this generation too had been covered by the earth, Zeus, son of Kronos, created yet another, a fourth, upon the fruitful land. They were more righteous and more valiant, a god-like race of heroes; 'half-gods' they are called, the age before our own upon the boundless earth. Harsh war and fearful battle destroyed some of them at the seven gates of Thebes, the land of Kadmos, as they fought over the flocks of Oedipus, and others it brought over the great gulf of the sea to Troy, because of Helen of the lovely hair. There death enfolded some for ever, but upon others Zeus the father, son of Kronos, bestowed life and dwelling apart from mankind, at the ends of the earth ...
>
> Then Zeus made yet another race of mortal men, who now exist upon the earth. If only I were not among the men of this fifth race! If only I could have died before them – or could be born after them! For this is now a race of iron; never do they rest from toil and sorrow by day, nor from wasting away by night; and the gods shall give them torment of mind.⁷⁰

Hesiod envisages the eventual destruction of this fifth race when violence and injustice will have made life intolerable for all but the strongest and most ruthless individuals. Yet he does not think of that as the end of man, as the second half of his wish, 'or could be born after them', shows. It would be interesting to know what he imagined would come next, but perhaps he did not turn his mind to that; for him the salient contrast is between the wretchedness of life as he knows it and the splendour of the 'half-gods' presented by poetry and myth. One of the achievements of the Greek historians was to sever legend from history and to focus their interest on what Herodotos⁷¹ called '*human* times'. This severance was tentative, partial and inconsistent, but it reflected a new awareness of the difference between a past which can profitably be studied and a putative past about which, in the last resort, one can only shrug one's shoulders.

Herodotos' way of working is illustrated by his account of the battle at the pass of Thermopylai, where a force of Spartans, supported by a contingent from Boeotia, held up the Persian invaders and – not a common event in the history of war – faithfully obeyed the command to fight 'to the last man'. The crisis came when the defenders' position had been bypassed and they could not withdraw.

> ... In this place they defended themselves with swords – those of them who still had swords – or with their hands and teeth, until at last some of the barbarians threw down the defensive wall and made a frontal attack, while others went round and assailed the Greeks from all sides. Then the Greeks were buried under a hail of missiles.
>
> Such was the courage of those men from Sparta and Thespiai; there is nevertheless one man who is said to have been bravest of all – Dienekes, a Spartan. There is a story about something he said before the battle with the Persians began. Told by one of the local people that when the barbarians fired their arrows, the number of shafts was so vast that the sun was hidden, he was not at all perturbed at that, but made light of the Persian numbers, saying, 'Our friend has brought us splendid news. If the Persians hide the sun, we shall be fighting in the shade.' They say that Dienekes the Spartan said quite a lot of things like that, which have been remembered after him.
>
> Next to Dienekes two Spartan brothers are said to have been the bravest, Alpheos and Maron, sons of Orsiphantes. Of the Thespians, a man called Dithyrambos, son of Harmatides, won the highest reputation.
>
> The dead were buried just where they fell, including those who died before the contingent sent away by [King] Leonidas departed. There is an inscription on their tomb, saying:
>
> > Here four thousand from the Peloponnese
> > fought against three millions.
>
> This inscription is for all the Greek dead, but there is a separate one for the Spartans:
>
> > Stranger, take word to Sparta:
> > here we lie, obeying her orders.[72]

This is stamped with the hallmark of Herodotos: 'one man who *is said* to have been bravest of all', '*there is a story* about something he said', '*they said* that Dienekes ... said ... a lot of things which *have been remembered*', 'two Spartan brothers *are said* to have been the bravest', 'Dithyrambos ... won the highest *reputation*'. Herodotos wrote the story of the Persian invasion of Greece, in the form in which we now read it, fifty years after it had happened. Unlike later historians, he could not work either from narratives compiled nearer the time or from archival material. He therefore had to make a synthesis of tradition, as it was told by men who had fought against the Persians and, at second hand, by the sons of those men. He understood that tradition is full of errors and distortions; the obstinate fact that two or more alternative traditions about the same event contradict each other confronted him at every stage. Sometimes he made a choice in accordance with his own predilections (we can see that he had a predilection for Athens and for democracy), or by applying criteria of probability which he does not disclose, as in:

The account I shall give of Cyrus accords with what is said by some Persians, those who do not want to magnify his life but tell the facts as they were; I could, however, give it in three other different ways.[73]

Or again:

Many different accounts are given of the death of Cyrus; the account I have given is the most plausible.[74]

But he does not always choose. He may give us a pair of conflicting accounts and renounce any attempt to reconcile them; and he explicitly forbids us to infer, from the fact that he tells a story, that he himself believes it:

I am obliged to tell what is told, but to believe it I am not entirely obliged, and that is to be taken as holding good for everything which I tell.[75]

We are now in a world quite different from that of the narrative books of the Old Testament. We have come into contact with the personal, individual judgement of Herodotos of Halikarnassos, treating tradition not as a sacred repository of truth but as material to be used in arriving at opinions. These opinions may at times go against the beliefs of the majority; there is no mistaking the undertone of polemic when Herodotos says:

In my opinion, Hesiod and Homer lived four hundred years, and not more, before my time.[76]

Greek historians were never afraid to use their own judgement. They were willing to say 'I don't know', to speculate about the motives of the people they described, and to qualify their opinions on occasion by 'perhaps' and 'probably'. It is the appearance of words like 'perhaps' which marks the beginning of true historical writing.

What made the Greeks write history was, pretty clearly, their capacity for being *interested* in things: interested not because the past could be made to reveal a divine purpose, but because it was – well, *interesting*. Then, as now, people were a little reluctant to admit that they studied something because they had an intellectual and imaginative appetite which clamoured to be fed. Herodotos contrives in his opening sentence to suggest that he writes out of a sort of obligation:

Herodotos of Halikarnassos here sets out the results of his enquiry, so that what has been done may not be obliterated by time from human memory and great and remarkable achievements, whether Greek or barbarian, may not lack the honour of remembrance; in particular, the reasons why Greeks and barbarians fought one another.[77]

One may indeed feel an obligation to rescue from oblivion actions which merit fame and serve as profitable models for imitation; but Herodotos' work is full of digressions – for example, on the animals of Libya or the customs of the Scythians – which cannot on any reckoning be classed as 'great and remarkable achievements'. Similarly, Thucydides, who belongs to the generation after Herodotos, professes to be concerned above all with the usefulness of his narrative:

> The absence of 'story-telling' in my work will perhaps diminish the pleasure of the listener; but if the work is judged useful by anyone who wishes to consider the truth of what has happened and what is likely (given the human situation) to happen on future occasions in similar or comparable form, that will be enough.[78]

Again, Thucydides is perfectly right in supposing that if we understand what has happened in the past we are better equipped to understand new situations, exactly as an individual is helped to cope with today by clear-headed scrutiny of the personal experiences which he went through yesterday; but over and above his austere purpose, Thucydides was a great writer who exploited to the full his gift for vivid and dramatic narrative.

Thucydides was an Athenian who suffered exile for a military failure which he did not consider to be his fault. He made a sustained effort (it did not come easily to him, and it was not invariably successful) to distance himself from the cities, people and events of which he wrote, to be neither 'pro-Athenian' nor 'anti-Athenian'. Herodotos, too, was a Greek who rejoiced proudly in the defeat of the 'barbarians' by his own nation, but he was true to the promise of his opening sentence: adulation and vilification were alien to him, barbarian courage and intelligence received proper tribute. It is not easy to imagine an Assyrian king saying on an inscription:

> I have set this up in order that the great and courageous achievements of my people and of my enemies the Elamites may receive due recognition.

The Assyrian, like the Jew, saw the hand of God in the outcome of battles. Thucydides did not; though he gives due weight to the religious motivations of commanders and peoples, he never commits himself to explanation in terms of the supernatural,[79] and he affords us an occasional glimpse of his own belief that events popularly regarded as supernatural interventions – a plague, an eclipse, a sudden storm – are in principle explicable in terms of scientific laws, however long we may have to wait for the details of the explanation. Herodotos did believe in gods, and he accepted the notion that they intervene in the course of events and in the fate of individuals; he did not doubt that it was the will of the gods that the Persian invasion of Greece should be defeated. Yet he is so far from turning his narrative into a sermon that he leaves the door ajar for science. So, for example, in speaking of a storm which fell upon the Persian fleet when it was anchored one night on its journey down the east coast of Greece:

> There is an account which says the Athenians called upon the North Wind, in accordance with an oracle...
>
> Now, whether it was for this reason that the North Wind fell upon the Persians at anchorage, I cannot say; the Athenians, at any rate, say that the North Wind had come to their aid before and that he brought about what happened on this occasion too...
>
> The storm went on for three days. In the end the Persian priests, by sacrificing victims and crying invocations to the wind, and in addition by sacrificing to Thetis and the Nereids, caused it to stop on the fourth day, or it abated of its own accord in some other way.[80]

Or should we say 'he abated of his own accord', with which the Greek text would be perfectly consonant? Perhaps Herodotos thought it unlikely that Thetis and the Nereids would have prevailed on the North Wind at the instance of the invaders. Perhaps he wondered why, if the North Wind answered the Athenians' prayers, he did not make a better job of it and destroy much more of the Persian fleet. Certainly he knew that no one could ask the North Wind why, or ever explain satisfactorily why a god acts or stops acting when he does. There are times when a firm seat on the fence is the only position compatible with intellectual honour, and Herodotos takes it when he is describing the geography of Thessaly:

> It is said that in earlier times the gorge and outflow of the Peneios did not exist, but these rivers, and Lake Boibeis in addition, not having the individual names they have now, flowed just as strongly as they do now and so made the whole of Thessaly an inland sea. Now, the Thessalians themselves say that [the god] Poseidon made the channel through which the Peneios flows, and what they say is plausible; for anyone who thinks that it is Poseidon who shakes the earth, and that clefts produced by an earthquake are the work of that god, would say, if he saw the Peneios gorge, that Poseidon had made it. The gap in the mountains certainly seemed to me to be the product of an earthquake.[81]

Just as Greek scientific speculation edged the gods out of the creation and working of the physical universe, so Greek historical interest edged the gods out of history. In both cases, the possibility of doing so existed because there was no central religious authority strong enough to stop it; and in both cases, the possibility was exploited because the Greeks were the kind of people they were. If gods intervene unpredictably and inexplicably, there is a limit to the usefulness of scientific explanation. Moreover, the study of human history becomes impracticable. Given some historical data, one poses questions and forms hypotheses in order to answer the questions. In forming the hypotheses, and above all in assessing

their relative probability, we rely on assumptions about human behaviour. We can do this because we know from our own experience what
it is like to be human. But we do not know what it is like to be a god,
and we cannot say what a god would *probably* do. That does not
stop many of us from making forthright assertions about what God will
have done or is bound to do, but such assertions must be ignored by
those who, like the readers for whom Thucydides wrote, 'wish to consider the truth of what has happened'. The assumption that supernatural
powers do not intervene in human history is a precondition of studying
it, and the Greeks were the first to take that assumption seriously.

### The Funny Side

Herodotos contained within himself the Greek nurtured on
poetry, accustomed from childhood to join with family and friends and
the whole community in prayer, sacrifice and festivals in honour of the
gods, and also the Greek aware that he was free to question anything and
to say what no one had said before. Sometimes we see one side of
Herodotos, sometimes another, but it is a matter of tilt only, not of
personalities in conflict within the same body. Few writers of any time
or place convey so strong an impression of an integrated and serene
personality.

The society of his day in civilised cities open to cultural and intellectual
influences from one another was not so serene or so well integrated. We
have seen what happened to Socrates, charged with 'corrupting the
young' and with 'not acknowledging the gods whom the city acknowledges'; and we have seen how Aristophanes constructed a 'Socrates'
out of scientific speculation, religious scepticism, venality, dishonesty and
cynicism. A gross, philistine piety, which could turn to fanaticism when
threatened, was one of the strands in the complex society of Athens
during the last third of the 400s BC.

While preparations for the Sicilian Expedition were going on in the
early summer of 415 BC, the statues of Hermes which stood everywhere
at the doors of private and public buildings in Athens were mutilated
during the night. The city was thrown into great alarm, for it was taken
for granted that Hermes would be angry and might bring the expedition
to ruin if those guilty of the offence could not be identified and killed
(there could be no question of a mere fine for a deliberate act of
sacrilege). Worse was to come: Alkibiades, one of the commanders of
the expedition, together with many of his acquaintances, was accused of
parodying the Eleusinian Mysteries for fun at private parties. To a
religious Athenian the Mysteries were of extraordinary importance; they
offered, through initiation in secret rituals, a way to security and privilege
in the after-life, and the fact that Eleusis stood on Attic soil gave Athens

a peculiar prestige. Such was the mood of the Athenians on hearing of these sacrilegious acts that informers, true or false, were readily believed, and men who were denounced fled if they could; in their absence they were condemned to death and all their property was confiscated by the state. We cannot, in the nature of the case, decide whether or not anyone had actually parodied the Mysteries at a party, but there is nothing intrinsically improbable about it; we know that some people at that time denied the existence of gods, and the parody was no doubt very funny. As for the statues of Hermes, *somebody* mutilated them, and the scale of the damage indicates that quite a number of people were involved. Whatever induced them to do it (and several more or less political motives have been suggested by historians), the one thing that can be said for sure is that they themselves did not fear the god's anger.

Denunciations, trials-in-absence and sentences of death continued throughout the second half of 415, and we know from some fragmentary inscriptions that public auctions of the confiscated property of the men condemned were still going on in the spring of 414. During this time Aristophanes composed the comedy *Birds* and had it produced at the City Dionysia. It is his longest, most spectacular play, and it presents us with two Athenians who have left Athens and gone to the land of the birds. One of the two, Peisetairos, persuades the birds to build a fortified city in the air, interposed between the realm of men and the realm of the gods. By this means they are able to prevent the smell of sacrificial roast meat from rising to heaven, and equally to prevent gods from nipping down to earth when a pretty girl has caught their eye. Their object is to force the gods to restore to them the rule of the universe which (or so Peisetairos has persuaded them) is theirs by ancestral right.

Zeus' first reaction is to send his messenger Iris to threaten Peisetairos with destruction. Peisetairos calls his bluff, refusing to recognise that Iris is a goddess and telling her with jocular ferocity that if she doesn't fly away he'll rape her. Iris does fly away, furious. The next god to arrive on the scene is Prometheus, and he comes as a traitor, cowering under a parasol to escape notice from above, in order to tell Peisetairos that an embassy will be coming from the gods to negotiate for peace. Prometheus is cast in this role because of his legendary quarrel with Zeus, told by Hesiod and dramatised by Aeschylus. Now he warns Peisetairos: don't make peace unless Zeus hands over his sceptre to the birds and gives you Basileia, 'Queen', the beautiful young housekeeper of the gods, in marriage.

When the embassy arrives, it consists of Poseidon, Herakles and a barbarian god, a 'Triballian' from Thrace, whose command of Greek is rudimentary. Peisetairos is supervising the cooking of a dinner.

POSEIDON (*to Herakles and the Triballian, in a declamatory style reminiscent of tragedy*): Now you see before you the fortress of Cloud-cuckoo-land, to which we come as envoys. (*To the Triballian*) What *are* you doing? You've got your cloak on left-ways round! Get it round – like this – to the right, can't you? Good God! You're as bad as Laispodias. O democracy! What will you bring us to in the end, if the gods have elected *this* one? (*He tries to adjust the Triballian's cloak properly*). Keep *still*! (*Giving up in despair*). Damn you! You're the most barbarous god I've *ever* seen! (*Turning to Herakles*) Well, now, Herakles, what are we going to do?

HERAKLES: I've told you already what *I* want to do. Strangle the man – whoever he is, the man who's walled off us gods!

POSEIDON (*patiently*): But Herakles – we've been elected as *envoys*, to *negotiate*.

HERAKLES: Strangle him twice over, that's what I say.

PEISETAIROS (*to his slaves*): Let's have the cheese-grater! Come on, some silphium! Bring the cheese, someone! Stoke up the charcoal!

POSEIDON (*pompously, to Peisetairos*): Greetings from the gods! We are an embassy of three.

PEISETAIROS (*without looking up*): Sorry, I'm grating the silphium for the roast.

HERAKLES: What kind of meat is it?

PEISETAIROS (*still without looking up*): Some birds conspired against the Democratic Republic of Birdland. They were condemned.

HERAKLES: So you grate silphium over them first?

[I am not at all sure what the humorous point of that line is. There may have been a traditional disagreement over whether silphium should be added before roasting the meat or after.]

PEISETAIROS (*noticing him at last*): Why, *Herakles*! Hul-*lo*! What's up?

POSEIDON (*with dignity*): We have come on an embassy from the gods to discuss terms for a cease-fire.

PEISETAIROS (*to a slave*): There's no oil in this flask!

HERAKLES: Yes, and bird-meat does need a bit of fat.

POSEIDON: *We* do not gain by continuation of the war; and if *you* were friends with us, the gods, you would have rain-water in your ponds and all your days would be halcyon days. We have come with full powers to conclude an agreement on the entire issue.

PEISETAIROS: Well, now, it wasn't ever we who started a war against you in the first place; and now, we're prepared – if it's agreed – if you're prepared, even now, to do something you ought to do – to make peace. And this is what is right and proper: Zeus must give his sceptre back to the birds. If we can conclude an agreement on those conditions, I invite the embassy to lunch.

HERAKLES: That's enough for me. I vote for it.

POSEIDON (*enraged, to Herakles*): *What?* You nincompoop, you guts! Will you deprive your father of his monarchy?

PEISETAIROS (*to all of them*): But, surely! Won't you gods be *stronger*,

if the birds rule down below you? As it is, mortals perjure themselves
by you because they're hidden under the clouds, but if you have the
birds as allies, whenever anyone swears by the raven and by Zeus,
the raven will be there, and he'll fly over to the perjurer and peck
out one of his eyes.

POSEIDON: By Poseidon, you've got something there!

HERAKLES: I think so too.

PEISETAIROS (*to the Triballian*): What do *you* say?

TRIBALLIAN: Ya, Beisatoo.

PEISETAIROS: You see? He agrees. Now, I'll tell you another good
thing we'll do for you. If a man vows a sacrifice to one of the gods
and then tries to wriggle out of it by saying 'The gods wait', and
doesn't give what's due, out of meanness, we'll exact what he owes.

POSEIDON: Why, how? Tell me.

PEISETAIROS: One day, when that man's counting out his money, or
sitting washing with his clothes off, a kite will fly down, without his
seeing, and grab the price of two sheep and bring it up to the god.
(*The gods go into a huddle, while Peisetairos gets on with his cooking*)

HERAKLES: I'm saying it again: I vote for handing over the sceptre to
them.

POSEIDON: Well, ask the Triballian.

HERAKLES (*menacing*): You, Triballian, do you want me to crack your
head?

TRIBALLIAN (*cowering*): You no 'it stick!

HERAKLES: He says I'm absolutely right.

POSEIDON (*to Peisetairos*): Sir! We agree to do as you said about the
sceptre.

In this portion of the scene Aristophanes has satirised negotiation in
a manner which has immediate appeal to anyone who has ever taken
part in it or shaken his head over it from the sidelines. X is persuaded
that he has been unjustly deprived of his rights by Y. So X goes to war
with Y. Y sues for peace. X sighs, 'Well, after all, *I* didn't start the war',
and then, magnanimously, 'All the same, even after all that's happened,
make just one concession, and I'm ready for peace'. Aristophanes at the
same time exploits the crude humour of foreigners' Greek, the folk-tale
image of Herakles as brutal, gluttonous and lecherous, the gods put out
of countenance. Poseidon is modelled on a well-to-do Athenian gentleman who finds himself, to his distaste ('O democracy!'), elected member
of a team whose manners are not his.

So far, we have heard nothing of the second demand which Prometheus
suggested to Peisetairos, marriage with Queen. Peisetairos has kept this
in reserve until the envoys from heaven have agreed to what he made
them think was his only demand. Now he goes on.

PEISETAIROS: Ah, now, there *is* another thing I've remembered! Hera

I concede to Zeus; but Queen – the girl – must be given to me in marriage.

The goddess Hera is Zeus' consort, so that here is a nice presumption in Peisetairos' concession (he says literally, 'Hera I hand over to Zeus'). At this point the negotiations nearly collapse, but Peisetairos' lunch invitation has had its effect on Herakles.

> POSEIDON: It isn't an agreement that *you* want! (*To Herakles and the Triballian*) Come on, let's be off home!
> PEISETAIROS: I don't mind. (*To a slave*) Cook! That sauce has got to be sweet!
> HERAKLES: Oh, Poseidon – what *is* the matter with you? Are we going to fight a war about one woman?

Herakles' words echo what many Greeks thought about the legendary Trojan War: all that, for one woman?

> POSEIDON: Why, what are we to do?
> HERAKLES: *Do?* Why, make peace!
> POSEIDON: My God! Don't you realise how you've been fooled all along? It's yourself that you're damaging! If Zeus hands over his monarchy to *them* and then dies, you'll be poor, because all his property, everything that Zeus leaves when he dies, comes to you.

At this point Peisetairos, who has kept his ear cocked, steps in and calls Herakles aside. He explains that Uncle Poseidon is deceiving him, because Herakles is son of Zeus by a mortal woman, a foreigner, so that (under Attic law) he wouldn't get a farthing of Zeus' estate anyway. An impressive quotation from the Laws of Solon and some fast, tricky arguments convince the slow-witted Herakles, who speaks up uncompromisingly.

> HERAKLES: I've thought all along that you're in the right about the girl, and I'm for giving her to you.
> PEISETAIROS (*to Poseidon*): Well, what do you say?
> POSEIDON: I vote against it.
> PEISETAIROS: It all depends on the Triballian. (*To the Triballian*) What do *you* say?
> TRIBALLIAN: Nice gorl big Queenie birdo me give.
> HERAKLES: He says, give her.
> POSEIDON (*exploding*): By God, *he* doesn't say anything about 'giving her', he's just twittering like the swallows!
> PEISETAIROS: Why, then, he says, give her to the swallows!
> POSEIDON (*faced by unmistakable defeat*): Well, you two come to terms and make the treaty. Since that's what you're both agreed on, I'll say no more.[82]

The parody of human negotiation is taken to its conclusion: when envoys appointed to a diplomatic mission, or (as happened with the Athenians at Syracuse) generals appointed to a joint command, could not be unanimous, the majority decision prevailed.

So Peisetairos, ordinary middle-class Athenian citizen, marries the ineffably beautiful housekeeper of the gods and takes from Zeus sovereignty over the universe.

The people who lashed out with death-sentences against men accused of mutilating statues or parodying the Mysteries gave a prize, in the same year, to the comic poet who made gods ridiculous on stage and created the fantasy of an astute human displacing the 'Father of Gods and Men'. It would not be true to say that comedy was licensed to make fun of *everything*. So far as our evidence goes, there was never a joke about the great plague which killed one third of the population of Athens in 430 BC; and amid very many jokes about sex and excretion, often expressed in the coarsest terms, there is none about menstruation or female homosexuality. Almost all aspects of religion could be satirised or ridiculed, but not absolutely all: there are no jokes against the Eleusinian Mysteries.[83] Nothing, it seems, must always be serious in all human cultures, and nothing must always be funny. Each culture is made to a unique recipe, for it is the product of its history and circumstances, and in that there can be no exact duplication. No one doubts that to understand any culture we must discover what it takes seriously. We need also to know what it finds funny, and how it uses laughter as a means of dealing with its predicaments and facing the next day.

### Last Words

A short book leaves out almost everything. This book is a handful of pebbles picked up from a long, bright beach and arranged in a sequence of my own choosing. Some of the questions on which I have made a confident statement in a dozen words, and some of the phrases I have translated (with no hint of alternatives) in the passages cited from Greek authors, have been the subject of many long articles in scholarly journals; and those articles have not been pedantic or nit-picking, but designed to take us a step or two nearer the truth in matters of importance to those who really care about what our fellow-humans at other times and places did, said, thought and felt. Reading what someone like me chooses to tell you about the Greeks is easy. To study the Greeks and form opinions which you can defend in detail is exacting. The reward is great, if Greek ways of seeing and saying are congenial to you.

It is inconceivable that they should be congenial to everybody. We all differ in our tastes, criteria and priorities, and some may see in Greek civilisation the root of what they dislike in ours. The Greeks were, after all, fiercely and deliberately competitive, believing that the whole community gains if it makes a fuss of those who excel and spurs the mediocre into doing their utmost by the threat of humiliation. They were also an extraordinarily articulate people, devoted to the structuring of art and utterance, contemptuous of immature and undisciplined self-expression. About competitiveness, I have misgivings; on structured articulateness, I side wholeheartedly with the Greeks. Most of my predilections have become obvious enough in the course of the book; it would have been odd if I had followed someone else's. My Greeks were neither sophisticated layabouts nor pious fatalists, and least of all were they portentous gurus brooding on the lost Secrets of the Ancients. They were resilient, sceptical, cheeky people, whose distinctive contribution to our history was to combine a readiness to ask 'Why?' and 'Why not?' with a conviction that only sane, reasoned and clearly expounded answers to those questions were worth listening to. I don't demand assent (I gave up demanding long ago), but I hope that you will entertain my picture of the Greeks beside other people's pictures of them and not put it away in the attic unless you are satisfied that it is incompatible with the evidence.

# Notes

1. (ed.) D. T. McLellan, *Marx's Grundrisse* (London 1920), pp. 44f.
2. *Leviathan*, Part II, ch. 21.
3. *Some Thoughts Concerning Education*, §174.
4. Eldrich Cleaver in (ed.) David Cooper, *The Dialectics of Liberation* (Penguin Books 1968), p. 154.
5. (ed.) James B. Pritchard, *Ancient Near Eastern Texts Relating to the Old Testament*, ed. 3 (Princeton 1969), p. 353.
6. *Iliad* iii 297–301.
7. S. Kramer, *The Sumerians* (Chicago 1963), p. 79.
8. (ed.) W. K. Simpson, *The Literature of the Ancient Egyptians*, ed. 2 (New Haven 1973), p. 22.
9. Pritchard, p. 367; Simpson, pp. 306f.
10. Pritchard, p. 208, §7.
11. I borrow the phrase from A. T. Olmstead, 'Persia and the Greek Frontier Problem', *Classical Philology* xxxiv (1939), pp. 305–322.
12. Roland G. Kent, *Old Persian: Grammar, Texts, Lexicon*, ed. 2 (New Haven 1953), p. 124.
13. Herodotos v 105.
14. Aeschylus, *Persians* 386–428.
15. Herodotos vii 10.e.
16. Plato, *Laws* 626a.
17. Xenophon, *Hellenica* vii 5.27.
18. Demosthenes ix (*Third Philippic*) 31.
19. Greek text in M. N. Tod, *Greek Historical Inscriptions* ii (Oxford 1948), pp. 224f.
20. L. W. King, *Assyrian Language* (London 1901), pp. 178–181.
21. Pritchard, p. 263.
22. Greek text in Russell Meiggs and David Lewis, *Greek Historical Inscriptions* (Oxford 1969), p. 62.
23. Thucydides ii 37.

24. Thucydides ii 63.2.
25. Thucydides ii 41.4.
26. Thucydides iii 40.4.
27. Thucydides iii 44.2.
28. Thucydides iii 36.4.
29. Thucydides vii 70.2; the next two passages quoted are 70.2–5 and 71.2 plus 71.4–6.
30. Thucydides vii 84.3–5.
31. Thucydides vii 87.1–2.
32. Thucydides vii 87.5–6.
33. Euripides, *Suppliants* 684–693.
34. The relevant evidence (in Greek) is in H. Diels, *Fragmente der Vorsokratiker*, revised by W. Kranz, sixth edition (Berlin 1951), Xenophanes A33.
35. Xenophanes B16.
36. Xenophanes B15.
37. Xenophanes B11 (cf. B12).
38. Xenophanes B23 and B24.
39. Hesiod, *Theogony* 27f.
40. Hesiod, *Theogony* 123–146.
41. *Fragmente der Vorsokratiker*, Anaximandros A30.
42. *Fragmente der Vorsokratiker*, Anaxagoras B17.
43. Theognis 731–752 (the sequence of short poems attributed to 'Theognis' includes material from the four hundreds, and this poem may belong to that period rather than to Theognis' own time).
44. The most vigorous and versatile period of Egyptian art had long passed by the time the Greeks got to know Egypt, and deliberate archaism had become an important element.
45. Christine Mitchell Havelock, *Hellenistic Art* (London 1971), pp. 22, 192.
46. *Odyssey* ix 375–443.
47. *Iliad* xxiv 33–54.
48. *Iliad* xxiv 56–63.
49. *Iliad* xxiv 486–512.
50. E.g. *The Triumph of Horus*, edited and translated by H. W. Fairman (London 1974).
51. *Agamemnon* 192–248.
52. *Agamemnon* 895–957.
53. *Agamemnon* 1089–1129.
54. *Libation-Bearers* 879–930.
55. Brian Vickers, *Towards Greek Tragedy* (London 1973), p. 1.
56. *Eumenides* 94–139.
57. Aristophanes, *Clouds* 366–394.
58. Plato, *Symposium* 215d–216a.

59. Plato, *Gorgias* 471e–472c.
60. Plato, *Apology of Socrates* 37e–38a.
61. Aiskhines, *Prosecution of Timarkhos* 173.
62. Plato, *Meno* 70a.
63. *Meno* 82b–86c.
64. *Fragmente der Vorsokratiker*, Protagoras B4.
65. *Fragmente der Vorsokratiker*, Kritias B25.9–15.
66. Plato, *Phaedo* 97b–e.
67. Plato, *Republic* 508c–509c.
68. *Fragmente der Vorsokratiker*, Demokritos B69, B264, B43, B45, B107a.
69. *Iliad* xii 447–9.
70. Hesiod, *Works and Days* 152–178.
71. Herodotos iii 122.2.
72. Herodotos vii 226–228.2.
73. Herodotos i 95.1.
74. Herodotus i 214.5.
75. Herodotos vii 152.3.
76. Herodotos ii 53.2.
77. Herodotos i, preceding 1.1.
78. Thucydides i 22.4.
79. There is a putative exception in ii 17.2, 'the oracle foresaw ...' (literally, 'the oracle knew in advance ...'), but what was foreseen was well within the province of ordinary human foresight.
80. Herodotos vii 189 and 191.2.
81. Herodotos vii 129.3–4.
82. Aristophanes, *Birds* 1565, 1645, 1674–84.
83. Aristophanes, *Frogs* 316–459 exploits and adapts for comic purposes some elements of a procession to Eleusis, but that is a different matter from treating the initiation rites themselves as funny.

# Further Reading

As I said in the Preface, this book does not attempt systematic coverage; it is essentially arbitrary in its selection of topics and its connection of thought. You can fill in the big gaps it has left, and encounter some views different from mine, in the following books:

(1) *General*
Three Pelicans, published by Penguin Books: A. Andrewes, *Greek Society* (1971), M. I. Finley, *The Ancient Greeks* (revised edition 1977) and H. D. F. Kitto, *The Greeks* (revised edition 1957).
   Two books in the series *The Making of the Past*, published by Elsevier-Phaidon: Alan Johnston, *The Emergence of Greece* (1976) and Roger Ling, *The Greek World* (1976).
(2) *History*
Two books in the series *Fontana History of the Ancient World* (Harvester Press): Oswyn Murray, *Early Greece* (1980) and J. K. Davies, *Democracy and Classical Greece* (1978).
(3) *Art*
John Boardman, *Greek Art* (Thames and Hudson, revised edition 1973).
(4) *Literature*
K. J. Dover and others, *Ancient Greek Literature* (Oxford University Press [OPUS series] 1980).
(5) *Myytholog*y
G. S. Kirk, *The Nature of Greek Myths* (Penguin Books 1974).

All the above will give you some guidance on books concerned with more specialised topics.
   At the same time as you are getting a firm grasp of the essential features of the ancient Greek world, it is a good idea to start reading Greek literature in translation. Most of it, including nearly all the works of the Classical period, is available in the *Penguin Classics* series. The *Loeb Classical Library*, published by Heinemann (in conjunction, now, with Harvard

University Press), has the Greek text and the English translation on facing pages; it is valuable for many authors of the later period, but in the case of most Archaic and Classical authors the Penguin translators have done better.

If you want to learn Greek and cannot join a class, I suggest the beginners' course *Reading Greek*, published by the Cambridge University Press for the Joint Association of Classics Teachers (1978); a teacher's help is desirable, but you *can* tackle the course on your own.

# Picture Credits

Acknowledgement is due to the following for permission to reproduce photographs:–

THE TRUSTEES OF THE BRITISH MUSEUM pages 26, 62, 63, 78 & 79; COLORPHOTO HINZ SWB colour plates 10, 11, 12, & 19; DELPHI MUSEUM (photo Tombazi) page 21; EKDOTIKE ATHENON S.A. front cover and colour plates 2, 8, & 41; EPIGRAPHICAL MUSEUM ATHENS pages 20 & 33; GERMAN ARCHAEOLOGICAL IN-STITUTE, ROME page 66; SONIA HALLIDAY colour plate 3; HIRMER FOTOARCHIV pages 48, 51, 53, 55 (right), 56, 59 (bottom), 60 & 80; KUNSTHISTORISCHES MUSEUM, VIENNA (photos Photo Meyer K.G.) colour plates 17a & b; NICO MAVROYENIS FOR BBC colour plate 1; G. MONTALBANO FOR BBC colour plates 5, 6 & 7; MUSEE DU LOUVRE, PARIS colour plate 18 and pages 57 (right), 82 & 83; SCALA colour plate 9; STAATLICHE ANTIKENSAMM-LUNGEN, MUNICH (photo C. H. Krüger-Moessner) colour plates 15a & b; STAATLICHE MUSEEN ZU BERLIN page 65; TAP SERVICE colour plate 14 and pages 54, 55 (left) & 61; UNIVERSITY OF ABER-DEEN, MARISCHAL COLLEGE page 57 (left).

Endpaper maps by Line and Line.

# Acknowledgements

Many helped to make the four television films, *The Greeks*.
We wish to thank especially:

National Directorate of Archaeology, Greece;
Italian Institute, London;
British Museum;
RM Productions; and

Charlotte Barshall: *Assistant Floor Manager*
Humphrey Burton: *Head of Music & Arts Department*
Kathryn Chavasse: *Production Secretary*
Steve Connelly: *Graphics Designer*
Linda Dalling: *Producer's Assistant*
Sidney Davies: *Film Cameraman*
Diana East: *Producer's Assistant*
Henry Farrar: *Film Cameraman*
Warwick Gee: *Film Operations Manager*
Ken Hains: *Dubbing Mixer*
David Jewitt: *Sound Recordist*
Doris Jordan: *Research Assistant*
John Keeping: *Assistant Film Cameraman*
Dave King: *Film Editor*
Roger Limb: *Producer, Radiophonic Music*
Terry Manning: *Film Electrician*
Dave Mason: *Film Electrician*
David May: *Film Grip*
Barry McCann: *Assistant Film Cameraman*
Michael McDermott: *Production Assistant*
Derek Medus: *Sound Recordist*
Carmella Milne: *Assistant Floor Manager*

ACKNOWLEDGEMENTS

Denis Moriarty: *Associate Producer*
Bruce Mullins: *Assistant Film Editor*
Naseem Nathoo: *Production Assistant*
Maria Powell: *Location Liaison*
Dacre Punt: *Designer*
Mike Sanders: *Stills Photographer*
Richard Somerset-Ward: *Assistant Head of Music & Arts Department*
Mike Southon: *Film Cameraman*
Jean Steward: *Make-up Artist*
Robin Swain: *Sound Recordist*
David Swan: *Assistant Film Cameraman*
Tony Vassilopoulos: *Greek Liaison*
Juanita Waterson: *Costume Designer*
Alf Williams: *Film Grip*

# Index

MACEDON

M. Olympos ✕

THESSALY

EUBO

Thermopylai ✕
M. Parnassos ✕
Delphi ●  BOIOTIA  Aulis ●
M. Helikon ✕
                Thebe ▣
ITHAKE        M. Kithairon ✕  Plataea ●
                Eleusis ●  ▣
        Corinth ▣
Olympia ●  ARCADIA  Mycenae ●  SALAMIS
Argos ▣  Epidauros ●  C. S
Tiryns ●

Sparta ▣

## GREECE
## AND THE AEGEAN